BERLITZ

DUBROVNIK
and Southern Dalmatia

1989/1990 Edition

D0493978

By the staff of Berlitz Guides
A Macmillan Company

How to use our guide

- All the practical information, hints and tips that you will need before and during the trip start on page 96.

- For general background, see the sections The Region and the People, p. 6, and A Brief History, p. 13.

- All the sights to see are listed between pages 20 and 73. Our own choice of sights most highly recommended is pinpointed by the Berlitz traveller symbol.

- Information on restaurants and cuisine is to be found on pages 74 to 82, while entertainment, nightlife and all other leisure activities are described between pages 83 and 95.

- Finally, there is an index at the back of the book, pp. 126–128.

Although we make every effort to ensure the accuracy of all the information in this book, changes occur incessantly. We cannot therefore take responsibility for facts, prices, addresses and circumstances in general that are constantly subject to alteration. Our guides are updated on a regular basis as we reprint, and we are always grateful to readers who let us know of any errors, changes or serious omissions they come across.

Text: Ken Bernstein
Photography: Daniel Vittet
We're particularly grateful to Sara Crowgey, Naum R. Dimitrijević, Karin Radovanović and Madge Tomašević for their help in the preparation of this book. We also wish to thank the Yugoslav National Tourist Office for their valuable assistance.
Cartography: Falk-Verlag, Hamburg

Contents

Cover picture: Dubrovnik

The Region and the People

Steep, forbidding mountains plunge into fragrant valleys, then down to a sea so transparent it's unfair to the fish. Nature has given Yugoslavia's southern Adriatic coast a bounty of bays and coves, Europe's longest children's beach and even an inlet as striking as a Norwegian fjord. Over many centuries, man has added citadels of stone which might have been transplanted from Venice or Constantinople.

This is a holiday region for all tastes. You can do the museums in the morning, lunch beside the sea (how about local

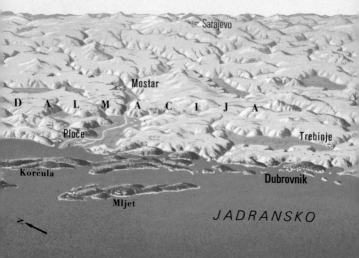

lobster and wine?), water-ski in the afternoon and listen to a symphony concert under the stars. You can stay in an ultra-luxury hotel with swimming pool, sauna, bowling alley, discotheque and gambling casino all under one fashionable roof. Or save your dinars and go native: rent a room in somebody's house at one-tenth the price.

An extra attraction for your curiosity is Yugoslavia's unique system of socialist self-government and its patchwork of nationalities, religions and languages. If you imagine hard-nosed bureaucrats, overbearing guides, travel restrictions or international intrigue, this is the wrong country. Foreign tourists receive an unqualified welcome in Yugosla-

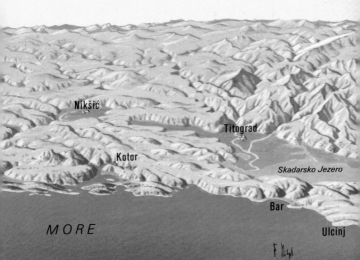

Nikšić

Titograd

Kotor

Skadarsko Jezero

Bar

MORE

Ulcinj

via; you're invited to go, do and see virtually everything —on your own.

As the dolphin swims, it's only 65 nautical miles from Dubrovnik to Ulcinj, Yugoslavia's southernmost coastal town.* This section of the *Jadranska magistrala* (Adriatic Highway) connects them over a twist-and-turn 194 kilometres. The area is part of two of Yugoslavia's six republics—Croatia and Montenegro. You'll know you've entered Montenegro when you notice street signs printed in Cyrillic letters.

Whether you encounter Croatians, Montenegrins or members of other Yugoslav

---

* Actually, Dalmatia runs from the island of Pag, north of Split, down to the Bay of Kotor, south of Dubrovnik. Our guide has also included the Montenegrin coast.

nationalities, you'll find them hospitable and proud. You'll want to see the real people in their own countryside, tending the vines and mending the fishing nets. Join them in the ritual promenade of early evening, supervised by the village elders at their café tables. Then taste the famed Dalmatian ham (*pršut*) on its home ground, and thank the ancient Greeks for the wine.

For the majority of tourists the sun-and-sand quotient has high priority. Frankly, much of the coast here is pebble or shingle. The swimming and

Fishermen work the clear Adriatic waters, home of hundreds of species. Right: local colour on a Dubrovnik street.

snorkelling excel, but beach purists may have to settle onto inflatable mattresses or deck-chairs.

The climate, on the other hand, could hardly be bettered anywhere. Twelve hours of sunshine is the daily mean in July—which outdoes the Mediterranean or Ionian islands. Yet the mean temperature (72–78° F in summer) is less oppressive than that of other paradises.

Not that life here is all sun and blue sky. When a summer storm comes, it can shake the world with time-exposure lightning flashes and drench it in Niagaras of rain.

An essential attraction of southern Dalmatia—indeed, one of the great sights of the world—is the city of Dubrovnik. Mighty stone walls and sophisticated diplomacy assured the freedom of this medieval city-state. You can trek the circumference of those walls today, inspect the bastions and look down upon ever-changing vistas of this sea-splashed "poem in stone". If you can't take prize pictures of these wonders under the sun, throw away your camera. Down at people-level, join the crowds strolling the Renaissance

Sunday in Ćilipi: old-time music through new-fangled microphones.

streets. Prowl the ancient palaces and churches for a whiff of history with your art. And try not to forget that these majestic plazas, these car-less, neon-less streets aren't the set for an epic motion picture but a real, lived-in city.

Dancers in everyday garb clasp hands in spontaneous kolo.

Southeastward from Dubrovnik, villages with charm and historic attractions of their own are trying to adapt to tourism. On the whole, the Yugoslavs have shown good taste and a respect for natural beauty in their development of the region. It was hard hit by the earthquake of 1979, but the process of reconstruction is almost complete.

Montenegro's coastal zone begins at the Bay of Kotor, south of Dubrovnik, appreciated since the Middle Ages for its cool grandeur and mild climate. The town of Kotor, hidden at the farthest reaches of the inlet, huddles between the sea and the grey eminence of Mount Lovčen. Behind its walls, the town remains a monument to centuries of architecture, engineering and art.

Beyond the Kotor area, the beaches roll on and on, far enough toward infinity to absorb almost any foreseeable increment in the tourist business. Along the way, the venerable walled town of Budva attracts crowds with its archaeological fragments, medieval architecture and lively modern pace. 11

One of the most fashionable resorts of Europe, Sveti Stefan, is a former fishermen's settlement on what was once an island but is now a peninsula. Its romantic medieval lanes and stone houses have been converted into a hotel-village. If they're fully booked or your budget won't let you stay the night, invest in a tour of its charming byways and swim from its twin crescent-shaped beaches.

Yugoslavia's southernmost seaside town, Ulcinj, mixes Turkish architecture and natural delights. Here, beneath the minarets, little boys with wide eyes wave at passing cars. Women in baggy trousers, masked by white shawls, lead donkeys down the road to market. Beyond the hilly city begins the longest sand beach on the Adriatic—more than seven miles—of uninterrupted, gentle dunes which dip gradually into the sea. If you're so inclined, test the curative properties of the sand which is credited with an uncommonly high iodine content. Addicts bury themselves in the radioactive sand (not going into the sea afterwards) and claim relief from lumbago and rheumatism.

This area beyond Ulcinj is a centre for nudists from many countries. Sunbathers with and without swimming costumes eye each other with curiosity but tolerance. They overcome their differences and coexist, like the Yugoslavs themselves.

Monuments, folklore, shopping ... but first, an Adriatic tan.

A Brief History

The history of Yugoslavia begins thousands of years ago. Yet its people have formed one nation only since 1918. And the very name of the country, Yugoslavia, became official even more recently.

The Adriatic shores were inhabited perhaps 5,000 years ago, long before the arrival of the Slavs. During the Bronze and Iron ages the Dalmatian Coast's tribes were Illyrians, probably the ancestors of present-day Albanians.

In the fourth century B.C., the dauntless Greeks set up trading posts on the mainland and nearby islands. By the first century A.D., the Romans had conquered both the Greeks and the Illyrians. Roman rule united the territory of Yugoslavia; ironically, this unification wouldn't be repeated until 1,500 years later.

The split in the Roman empire toward the end of the fourth century changed the fate of the entire ancient world, not least of all the Balkans. What are now Serbia, Macedonia, Montenegro and most of Bosnia-Herzegovina were tilted into the Eastern empire of Con-

St. Blaise, Dubrovnik's patron.

stantinople; the Western empire gathered Slovenia and Croatia (with Dalmatia) under the wing of Rome. The cultural and religious division was reinforced in the Middle Ages when the western, Catholic regions fell under Austro-Hungarian or Venetian rule, while the eastern, Orthodox parts 13

Adriatic fortress-cities were the answer to constant assaults.

were swallowed up in the Turkish empire. Despite political unification in modern times, the division has never been totally erased.

The Dark Ages

The Dark Ages were harsh in Yugoslavia. Hordes of invaders scourged the land. Some came from infamous barbaric tribes like the Goths, Huns and Vandals. No less menacing were the Avars, founders of the first Mongol empire. Among the soldiers attached to the Avar armies may have been the first Slavs to set foot in Yugoslavia around the middle of the sixth century. From plunder the invaders

gradually turned to more homely occupations, such as settling down with the locals in communes. (The extended family unit thus created remained a legally recognized organism until the 19th century.)

But domestic tranquillity was doomed by the turbulence of the times. New invasions and big-time power politics wrenched apart the territory of Yugoslavia.

In A.D. 924—a time of scandal and skulduggery in Rome —Pope John X crowned Tomislav the first king of Croatia. The kingdom managed to survive for nearly 200 years, whereupon Hungary took direct control over the fate of the

Croatians. Meanwhile, competing feudal lords chopped the Dalmatian Coast into bits. Each city bowed before its own separate destiny; the ups and downs of the principal towns are detailed later in this book.

Thanks to sea-power, diplomacy and a notorious 100,000-ducat land deal, most of the Coast soon came under the control of Venice. Art and architecture flourished but it was an era of political doldrums. The future was passing Venice by. Although the Venetians didn't realize it at the time, Columbus changed their world. By reducing the importance of Mediterranean trade routes, he greased the skids for the republic's 300-year slide to decay and ruin.

Serbian and Turkish Power

In Serbia, the kingdom of the Nemanjić dynasty emerged in the 13th century as the most powerful state in the Balkans. Its wealth and advanced cultural level can be judged from the innumerable Orthodox monasteries and churches with their fresco-covered interiors, built by the kings and other nobility of the age throughout Serbia and Macedonia.

Doorway on island of Korčula: memories of Venice's heyday.

The realm of Emperor Dušan the Mighty stretched from the Danube to the Aegean. But after his death in 1355 internal power struggles weakened the state, which gradually fell a prey to Turkish encroachments from the Ottoman em- 15 pire. Serbia's fate was sealed by its crushing defeat at the Battle of Kosovo in 1389. Though the process took another century, the Ottoman empire finally gained complete control over Serbia, Bosnia, Herzegovina and Macedonia.

As the Ottoman empire decayed and the central government lost its grip, Turkish rule grew repressive. In Bosnia and Herzegovina, in particular, many Slavs were converted to Islam; the Moslem way of life took deep root. Even in other regions, the Turkish influence can still be noticed in the architecture, crafts, cooking, music and national costumes.

Serbia and Montenegro freed themselves from Turkey to become independent principalities (later kingdoms) in the mid-19th century. Soon after, Bosnia-Herzegovina fell under Austro-Hungarian control which lasted until 1918. Macedonia remained Turkish until as recently as the Balkan War of 1912.

For all their power elsewhere, the Turks never conquered the coast. They did, however, threaten Venetian rule, periodically attacking its cities. Dubrovnik paid tribute to the sultan to survive.

With the subjugation of the Venetian republic by Austria in 1797, the Hapsburg empire assumed its long and tumultuous rule over the coastal zone.

Napoleonic Influence

One dramatic interruption was Napoleon's seizure of Dalmatia in 1809. With nostalgia for ancient history, he renamed the territory the Illyrian Provinces. This long view was scant con-

Film company in Sarajevo re-stages archduke's ill-fated 1914 visit.

solation for the proud citizens of the republic of Dubrovnik who were bundled into the French scheme by the overwhelming force of arms. For the first time in hundreds of years of independence, the city-state was occupied by foreign troops. When Napoleon, suffering from his Russian hangover, abandoned Illyria in 1815, it was too late for Dubrovnik to regain its sovereignty; the Austrians became the new masters.

Further south, Napoleon had also occupied the Bay of Kotor region. His defeat fertilized a new flowering of Montenegrin nationalism, and the mountain principality, which had tenaciously and more or less successfully resisted Turkish conquest for centuries, at last achieved an outlet to the sea. But the Great Powers quickly vetoed this, handing the spoils again to Austria. Over the next century many nationalist uprisings harrassed the occupiers but the Austrians were able to suppress them every time.

The Austrian connection with Yugoslavia was to change the history of the world. On June 28, 1914, Archduke Francis Ferdinand, heir to the Hapsburg empire, was assassinated in the Bosnian city of Sarajevo. The Serbian government was accused of connivance in the plot. After issuing a humiliating ultimatum which Serbia couldn't accept and urged on by a Germany which believed in dealing from strength, Austria-Hungary declared war, hoping to expand its Balkan territories. The other big powers were drawn in, and Europe marched into the horrors of World War I.

After heroically checking the Austro-Hungarian advance for over a year and, incidentally, winning the first allied victory of the war at Cer, the exhausted Serbian armies, weakened by a typhoid epidemic, short of supplies and attacked from the rear by Bulgaria, were forced to retreat across the Albanian mountains to Corfu. It was here that the concept of a united Yugoslavia, the long-cherished dream of Southern Slavs, formally took shape. In mid-summer 1917, representatives of Serbia, Croatia, Slovenia and Montenegro signed the Corfu Declaration calling for the formation of a single state under the Serbian crown in which all Yugoslav peoples would enjoy complete equality. 17

Tumultuous Search for Unity

The years between the world wars made Yugoslavia the kind of country which inspired clichés about the Balkan tinderbox. Italian troops, implementing a secret treaty of 1915 in which Britain, France and Russia promised these regions to Italy as part of its reward for joining the allies in the war, occupied Istria and parts of the Dalmatian coast. In addition, failure by the Serbian-dominated government to meet the terms of the Corfu Declaration regarding national equality was a source of bitterness and discord within the young state. In 1928, the Croatian opposition leader was shot down in parliament; the following year King Alexander proclaimed a royal dictatorship, banning all political parties and nationalist organizations. It was at this time the country's name was changed to Yugoslavia. The world depression of the early 1930s was particularly hard on Yugoslavia's economy; the unemployment rate boiled to an explosive 40 per cent. In 1934, on a state visit to France, King Alexander was assassinated by a killer working for Macedonian and Croatian separatist groups.

Staggered by these disasters, and surrounded by the growing menace of Hitler and Mussolini, Yugoslavia tried to steer clear of Europe's approaching confrontations. But protestations of neutrality couldn't match the pressures. In March 1941, Prince Paul, the regent, went to Hitler's Berchtesgaden hideaway for a secret audience with the *Führer*. The resulting agreements pledged Yugoslavia's support for the Axis in return for the promise of Salonika (Greek Macedonia). Irate Yugoslavs sent Paul packing into exile within a matter of days. Under popular pressure, the new government renounced the Axis pact so enraging Hitler that he declared he would wipe Yugoslavia off the map.

On April 6, 1941, without a formal declaration of war, the *Luftwaffe* bombed Belgrade; Axis troops rolled across five frontiers. Ill-prepared and betrayed, the defending armies of young King Peter, capitulated within ten days. As Peter and his top men fled to exile, Yugoslavia's foes swooped on the luckless country. Germany, Italy, Bulgaria, Hungary and Albania dismembered most of the territory; the remainder fell under the rule of collaborators.

But the vanquished struck back. Guerrilla bands soon organized large-scale resistance activities. Initially, in 1941 the communist-led Partisans and royalist Chetniks under Col. Draža Mihailović agreed to join forces against the enemy. But it soon became apparent that they were too incompatible politically to cooperate. Evidence increased that Chetniks were assisting the Germans against the Partisans, and by 1943 the allies were dropping supplies only to the Partisans' National Liberation Army, commanded by Josip Broz Tito. The triumphant uphill fight of the Partisans in pinning down tens of thousands of enemy troops and finally liberating their own country has been widely told. The price the Yugoslavs paid for their liberty was high–the loss of over 1,700,000 lives.

Photo: Hans Keusen

President Tito in 1949, a forceful and independent leader.

A Republic Proclaimed

At the end of 1943, Tito was named marshal of Yugoslavia and president of the National Liberation Committee (a provisional government). As peacetime leader of a new Yugoslavia–proclaimed a socialist federal republic on November 29, 1945–he totally altered the course of his country's economic and political life. In 1948 Yugoslavia broke with Stalin, abandoning Soviet tutelage to create a distinctive brand of socialism based on worker management and self-governing communes. The vexing nationalities question was met by giving each of the six republics almost complete autonomy in its internal affairs. The foreign policy of non-alignment (of which Tito was a founder) catapulted Yugoslavia to an international significance far beyond its size or wealth. With the death of Tito in 1980 Yugoslavia turned to the task of consolidating the real-life achievements of the legendary national leader.

19

Where to Go

Dubrovnik
Pop. 66,000

This magnificent city of cold marble warms the heart. The centuries-old perfection of the setting between a lush mountainside and a limpid sea radiates a sense of harmony and well-being. Preserved behind unconquered walls, Dubrovnik is ingenious and impeccable.

When the Slav and Avar tribes were pillaging the area in the seventh century, they swooped down on the very civilized Roman town of Epidaurus (later Cavtat). Survivors of the sack of Epidaurus took refuge on an islet a few miles up the coast. Slavs settled a stone's throw across the nar-

row channel but peace ensued. In the Middle Ages the islet was linked to the mainland; what had been the strait became Dubrovnik's main street.

Dubrovnik, formerly known as Ragusa, evolved its independence under foreign influence —first Byzantine, then Venetian and later that of the Croato-Hungarian Kingdom which began to exercise loose control in 1358. The city's individuality was asserted early. In the 14th century Ragusa minted its own currency. In the 15th it abolished slavery, inaugurated social services and began a network of diplomatic ties. Soon the autocratic yet surprisingly progressive city-state was a power to contend with. In exchange for heavy payoffs, the Ottoman empire gave Dubrovnik the green light for triumphs of trade and diplomacy. The tiny republic enjoyed a commercial monopoly between East and West. Admiration or envy over Dubrovnik's mercantile achievements created the poetic English word for an adventurous merchant ship, "argosy", derived from "Ragusa".

Freedom and prosperity permitted art and scholarship to thrive within the fortress walls. But then came the city's darkest day—April 6, 1667. A catastrophic earthquake killed perhaps 5,000 people and devastated most of Dubrovnik's architectural gems. The proud city was rebuilt but declining economic conditions hampered a full recovery. Re-

Tourists enjoy aerial view of Dubrovnik and Lokrum island.

minders of the disaster are still in evidence around the city; 1667 is the accepted dividing line between the glorious old days and modern times.

On May 26, 1806, the French army occupied Dubrovnik. The republic's diplomatic agility couldn't blunt the harsh blow of history. Dubrovnik became a tributary state of the Illyrian Provinces of Napoleon's dreams. Worse was soon to come. Nine years later, under the Treaty of Vienna, Dubrovnik was given to the Austrians for another century of imperial rule.

But the cherished remnants of the age of liberty went on to proclaim the glory that was Ragusa. This gracious greatness is what appeals today to the thousands who thrill at encountering this living past.

Most tourists approach the old city from the western suburb of Pile, with its bus stops, taxi stands, travel agencies and traffic jams. You'll walk across a wooden drawbridge and through the Gothic arch of the **Pile gate.** (You can't drive; motor vehicles are banished from the old city.) Set over the arch is one of a number of sta-

Pile gate: boundary between modern and medieval Dubrovnik.

tues of St. Blaise, the patron saint of Dubrovnik. A thousand years ago, it's said, his miraculous warning staved off a Venetian attack.

The **city walls,** among the world's most imposing and best preserved medieval fortifićations, have a circumference of about one and a quarter miles and are up to 18 feet thick. Stone defences were first constructed as early as the seventh century; fragments remain from the tenth century. But what surrounds the city today essentially dates from the 15th and 16th centuries. The battlements include 15 towers, 5 bastions, 2 corner towers and a fortress.

For a small admission charge you can follow in the footsteps of the sentries of old for all or part of the circuit of the walls and imagine the moat which once existed. In addition to a close look at the fortifications, you'll find new perspectives over the pale tile roofs of the city and the sea. The best view is from the highest tower, **Minčeta,** at the northwest corner of the wall. This great round fortress, begun in the 14th century, is one of the symbols of the former strength of this ancient city-state.

The town plan evident from the elevated view also strikes the traveller entering on foot. There's only one main street, and it's undisputedly grand. The **Placa** (pronounced PLAT-sa) was built over the sea channel which once separated the halves of the city. The stone paving, scuffed smooth by centuries of sandals and boots, cries out to be strolled upon. In disciplined ranks, four-storey houses, always of stone, balance the street. Their ground floors are mostly assigned to commerce, unpretentious façades subtly playing down the

Where ancient sentries paced.

town's business centre. Most shops retain the distinctive Dalmatian architectural tradition of the arched door-and-window combination, known as the *na koljeno* ("onto the knee") style. Today the door-and-a-half design is rarely used for handing over purchases onto the customer's knee. But visitors to Dalmatia agree that it's an attractive relic.

Although the design of the Placa goes back to the 13th century, a great proportion of its buildings were destroyed or gravely damaged in the 1667 earthquake. Thus most of

Dubrovnik's Placa: perfection in stone, throbbing with life.

the Gothic and Renaissance touches were replaced by baroque façades. The simple, harmonious whole remains.

During the day, the Placa is abustle with tourists and locals on shopping sprees and errands. The shops observe a long lunch-and-siesta break during which the city relaxes into tropical lassitude. In the early evening the street becomes the setting for the traditional *korzo,* a time for chatting, flirting, ambling and gaping. The area is so animated that it all sounds like an immensely successful, monster cocktail party.

A landmark and rallying point at the western end of the Placa is a 16-sided, domed reservoir known as **Onofrio's Great Fountain.** Onofrio della Cava, a Neapolitan architect, built Dubrovnik's 15th-century water-works: a seven-mile aqueduct system from mountain springs to city fountains. This one, the biggest and most prominently placed, lost many decorative touches in the 1667 earthquake.

An earlier tragedy, the quake of 1520, is commemorated at the first church inside the western wall. Miraculously, the tiny **Our Saviour's church** (*crkva Sveti Spas*) escaped damage in the 1667 upheaval, one of the few buildings spared. Its Renaissance façade and Gothic interior make it a rare, intact example of Dubrovnik's noblest age of harmony and workmanship, which was cut short by the earthquake.

A fountain and rendezvous point.

Next to Sveti Spas, and over-shadowing it, the **Franciscan church** is entered through a lavish principal portal, facing the Placa. This is a late Gothic ensemble from 1499. The bright interior of the church was reconstructed after the 1667 disaster. The **cloister** of the Franciscan monastery alongside escaped the quake. This early 14th-century complex by Mihoje Brajkov of Bar encloses a lush garden with elegance and even a touch of eccentric humour. Each arcade of the cloister consists of six tall arches supported by twin columns. The capital of each pair of octagonal columns comprises different sculptures —gargoyles, comedy and trage-dy masks or caricatures. Next door, a **chemist's shop** (or drugstore)—one of the oldest in Europe—has been restored, down to the last apothecary jar and pestle. The 1317 chemist's is a down-to-earth, yet beauti-ful, reminder of the workaday world of the Middle Ages.

At the far end of the Placa, the pigeons panic every time the municipal **clock tower** sounds the hour. You can watch replicas of 15th-century bronze clappers in the form of soldiers striking a 16th-century bell. The "green men" in the belfry are symbols of Dubrov-nik. The tower itself was re-constructed in modern times.

A few yards away is another achievement of the water-works man, Onofrio della Ca-va. **Onofrio's Small Fountain** is an imaginatively sculpted, cheerful souvenir from the mid-15th century. And it still works.

In the centre of the square, **Orlando's column** reflects the reality of the republic of Ragu-sa. In the Middle Ages, govern-ment decrees were proclaimed from the top of the column; malefactors received public punishment at its base.

In a city so well endowed with churches, one might be tempted to slight the **church of St. Blaise** *(Sveti Vlaho)* on the same square. This chapel-size edifice, dedicated to the city's patron saint, is scarcely an-tique by local standards. It was built in the early 18th century. But inside, behind the altar, a 15th-century, silver-gilt sta-tuette portrays St. Blaise him-self. The elaborately robed effi-gy is holding a model of the walled town of Dubrovnik, a municipal portrait so accurate that it might have been based on an aerial photograph.

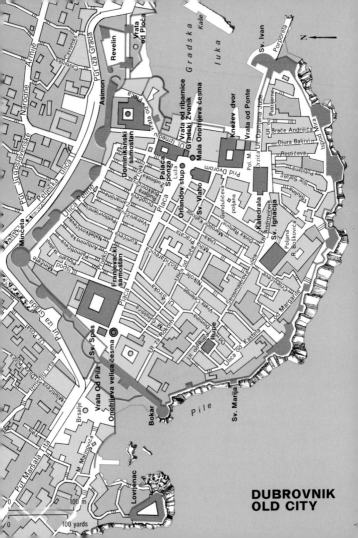

DUBROVNIK
OLD CITY

Opposite the complicated façade of the church stands the **Sponza Palace,** one of the most unusual and attractive buildings in Dubrovnik. Architect Paskoje Miličević blended Gothic and Renaissance styles —gracefully arched arcades, intricate tracery on tall, gothic windows on the floor above and square windows on the top storey. This was the republic's customs house and later served as the mint. Now it contains the state archives as well as the Museum of the Socialist Revolution.

Behind the Sponza Palace, and not far from Ploče gate *(Vrata od Ploča)* is the compound of the **Dominican monastery.** A church stood here in the early 14th century but reconstructions after various disasters have left little of the original. The simple interior includes a Titian painting as well as examples of religious art by local artists of the 15th and 16th centuries. The monastery's cloisters retain the meditative charm for which they were designed 500 years ago, with slender arches within arches, a Renaissance well and tropical flora.

The history and beauty of Dubrovnik are admirably com-bined in the **Rector's Palace,** the city's most impressive structure. It was designed by Onofrio della Cava (who also did the noted fountains): a stately portico, Gothic windows above and, inside, a perfectly proportioned courtyard with a grand staircase to an arcaded balcony. (The Dubrovnik Symphony Orchestra gives concerts in the atrium three nights a week; the music takes on a special dimension because of the classic setting.) This palace was the residence and ceremonial office of the rector of the ancient republic of Ragusa. The aristocrats of Dubrovnik took turns at the job of ruling, each with a one-month term of office. During his tenure, the rector was admonished, as the Latin inscription over the portal of the Great

Council puts it, to "forget private affairs and concern yourself with civic matters" *(obliti privatorum publica curate)*. The council chamber and adjoining halls are now given over to a museum of Dalmatian art. There is also a numismatic collection.

A final landmark in this glance at the historical highlights of old Dubrovnik: the baroque **cathedral**. It replaced a 12th-century church destroyed in the 1667 quake. (A legendary blessing said to have been offered at the start of construction by Richard the Lion-

Left: *Medieval whimsey is reflected in the columns of the cloister of the Franciscan monastery. Below: Grace and grandeur in classic courtyard of Rector's Palace.*

heart seems to have been in-effective in guarding the structure.) The "new" cathedral houses some notable works of art. A large polyptych of the Assumption is signed by Titian. A priceless collection of reliquaries in the cathedral's treasury is open at restricted

Market scene at ancient wall.

hours. Among the exhibits is a 12th-century Byzantine crown said to contain part of the skull of St. Blaise. This elaborate crown and other relics are borne in solemn procession every year on the feast day of the city's patron saint. Intensive excavations beneath the cathedral have uncovered the remains of a Byzantine church, including beautiful frescoes, shedding new light on the history of the town.

Between the cathedral and the Rector's Palace, the gate called Vrata od Ponte goes through the great wall to the **old harbour.** Nowadays it handles only the smaller craft —local ferryboats, fishing boats and a few yachts. Once it was an important port, shipbuilding centre and arsenal, protected not only from storms but from potential foes. Huge iron chains could be stretched between the fortresses and the ingenious 15th-century breakwater to thwart unwelcome warships. All today's maritime activity can be watched at leisure from the terrace of a café *(Gradska kavana)* which overlooks the scene.

As early as the 16th century Dubrovnik had outgrown the old harbour. The main port moved to Gruž, about two miles to the west. This is where the passenger liners, freighters and most of the pleasure boats put in. Shuttle buses link Gruž with the terminus at Pile, just outside the ancient city walls.

Before you leave the old town, spare some time to wander beyond the vital spots covered in guide books or on the group tours. Mingle in the market where the fruit of the land and fish fresh from the sea advertise themselves. Escape the hubbub to cool back streets where old women embroider just out of range of the drip of the day's laundry drying in the morning sun. Climb the steep

Excursion boat sails from 500-year-old port.

stepped-streets at random to discover the all-but-hidden churches, mansions, gardens, sculpture and forgotten delights of time-worn stonework. These obscure, unglamourous streets may not be important enough to attract the crowds, but they prove that life really goes on today much as it did in Dubrovnik's grandest age.

Then take the cable car up the mountainside for a thrilling bird's-eye view. If you go up late in the afternoon you can watch the roofs, the sea and the sky catch the light as an apricot-coloured sun descends amid the islands into the deep-blue Adriatic.

Meštrović statue honours hero of Montenegro, ruler Peter II.

Whittling to Greatness

Ivan Meštrović grew up in a Dalmatian mountain village in the 1890s, carving wood and stone to pass the time while he tended sheep. Today his sculptures are considered modern classics. They include Belgrade's tomb of the unknown soldier and Chicago's statue of an Indian on horseback.

Meštrović learned the rudiments at 15 from a master mason in Split. After art school in Vienna, he opened a studio in Paris, under the influence of Auguste Rodin. In the years after World War II, Meštrović taught at Syracuse (New York) University and finally at Notre Dame University in Indiana. He died, a naturalized American citizen, in South Bend, Indiana, in 1962.

His heroic or simple-yet-powerful works brighten up many a Yugoslavian church, courtyard or museum, from sea-level at Dubrovnik to the top of Mount Lovćen.

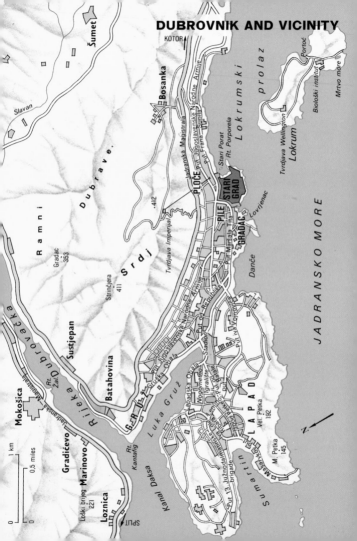

DUBROVNIK AND VICINITY

Island Hopping

More than a thousand islands, rocks and reefs pierce Yugoslavia's Adriatic waters. Most are barren protuberances as unromantic as the geology samples they resemble. But quite a few are substantial, developed paradises.

With Dubrovnik as the launching pad you can reach several of the most desirable islands by local ferryboat or on organized day-trips. The highlights:

LOKRUM is just a 15-minute ferry hop from the old harbour of Dubrovnik. Legend links Lokrum with Richard the

Pine-wooded Lokrum, one of Yugoslavia's 1,000 Adriatic isles.

Lion-hearted. Although modern research tends to dismiss the story, the valiant English king is said to have been shipwrecked here on his way back from leading the Third Crusade in 1191. Regardless of the truth, Lokrum would be a most welcome port in a storm. It's been preserved as a national park, ideal for rambles through the pinewoods, for picnics and swimming.

If Dubrovnik sightseeing hasn't exhausted your interest in historical buildings, consider Lokrum's abandoned Benedictine monastery. Begun in the 11th century, it was built in slow stages covering at least four distinct architectural eras. Nearby is the royal residence built in the last century by Archduke Maximilian of Austria, who less than a decade after its completion was executed in 1867 by the Mexicans he endeavoured to rule. The monastery serves as a natural-history museum, complemented by a botanical garden of subtropical plants. There's also a small museum dedicated to the Dubrovnik mathematician and astronomer Rudjer Bošković whose birthplace is right next to Dubrovnik's Sponza Palace.

At the island's summit, the ruins of a star-shaped fort recall the French occupation at the beginning of the 19th century. At the south end of the island, a small salt lake bears the evocative name of Mrtvo More ("dead sea").

To the northwest of Dubrovnik stretches an archipelago called the Elaphite Islands. The closest—less than half an hour by ferryboat—is Kolo-ČEP. A few hundred people carry on fishing and sailing as the island's ancient Greek and Roman settlers did. A parish church built between the 13th and 15th centuries is better preserved than most of the island's monuments—such as the

Unaccustomed seaside sun imperils tender skin from northern climes.

ruins of anti-pirate fortifications and the crumbling summer residences of the old nobility. Nature is almost totally unspoiled with sandy or shingle beaches and thick pine forests to explore.

The most developed of the Elaphite chain, LOPUD, is a tourist resort with a distinguished past. At one time it's thought that as many as 14,000 people lived on the island when it held special status under the Dubrovnik republic. Its most solid citizen was the 16th-century merchant prince, Miho Pracat, who bequeathed

his entire fortune to the republic. A bust of the philanthropist stands in the courtyard of the Rector's Palace in Dubrovnik—the only monument to a private or public citizen the city-state ever erected.

Lopud itself has a vice-rector's palace—not so grand as its mainland equivalent but still a good example of the era's architecture. And it's all wrapped up in a subtropical garden. Sightseers can find other indications of the island's past importance in the remains of castles, a monastery and many luxurious villas.

A mild tourist boom has roused Lopud from its long doldrums but the modern hotels and restaurants don't significantly encroach on the island's verdant beauty.

The island of ŠIPAN (about six and a half square miles) is the largest of the Elaphites. It offers a couple of quaint villages and a valley rich in oranges and lemons, grapes and olives. Wanderers will come upon ancient churches, most notably the remains of the 11th-century St. Peter's church. The unusual, much-fortified Holy Spirit church *(crkva Sveti Duh)* was constructed to face the perils of

On the waterfront at Lopud.

the mid-16th century. The same era produced two large towers for defence against pirate raids and the summer residence of the archbishop of Dubrovnik.

One of the Adriatic's loveliest islands, **Mljet,** is a favourite destination for Dubrovnik day-trippers. Prehistoric ruins indicate that its natural attractions have been enjoyed for thousands of years. At about 38 square miles, Mljet is the largest, as well as the prettiest, island in the Dubrovnik area. Thick Aleppo pine forests cover most of it, but there are vineyards and olive groves as well.

About 7,400 acres are set aside as a national park. Tourist facilities are limited. The most atmospheric choice is a Class-B hotel converted from a 12th-century Benedictine monastery. The setting is incomparable: on the edge of a small islet in Veliko Jezero ("great lake"), one of two linked salt lakes. Visitors to the islet, called Melita, have a choice of archaeological sights, rambles and superb bathing off the rocks. You can walk all the way around the fragrant isle in less than 10 minutes.

On rustic Šipan, the islanders still outnumber the tourists.

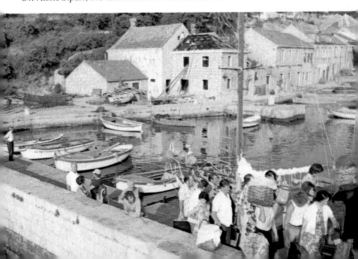

Triumph of medieval town planning: stone city of Korčula.

🏃 Cruise to Korčula

A popular day trip from Dubrovnik is an organized cruise to the wooded island of Korčula. The voyage by hydrofoil takes about one hour and 40 minutes each way. Or you can go by steamer, enjoying the scenery en route, then returning to Dubrovnik by bus. But the hydrofoil cruise leaves a lot more time for sightseeing ashore.

Korčula is the longest island in southern Dalmatia. Its area —107 square miles—is almost the size of Martha's Vineyard in Massachusetts or a bit smaller than the Isle of Wight. The mainland of Yugoslavia (actually the slim Pelješac peninsula) is less than a mile away.

Famous for its wine and mild climate, Korčula is especially proud of its principal city of stone construction, an inspiration of medieval town planning. The streets of the cramped island follow a herringbone layout ingeniously arranged to baffle the wind. Religious and administrative buildings in Gothic and Renaissance style give the squares and lanes a serene grace.

Korčula's history just might extend as far back as the 12th century B.C., when, legend says, it was settled by the Trojans. In any case, Greek colonists lived there as early as the fourth century B.C.; it was then that the island's first coins were minted. About 33 B.C. Korčula was brutally Romanized by Octavian Augustus, the emperor who rejected the advances of Cleopatra. In the ninth century A.D.–after about three centuries of Byzantine rule–the island was settled by Croats from the Dalmatian mainland. The Venetians conquered Korčula in the well-rounded year of 1,000 and held on—except for some tumultuous intervals–for nearly eight centuries.

At the beginning of the 19th century the island bowed to a succession of heavyweight rulers: Austria, Britain, France and Russia. The British contributed the brooding 1815 fortress (Fort Wellington) on the hill overlooking the old town.

During World War II, Korčula changed hands tragically. The Italians held the island initially, then they were driven off, only to be replaced by the Germans, who controlled Korčula until the final liberation in September 1944. In addition to the heavy loss of life, the fighting damaged historic buildings. But enough has been preserved

---

Island Menageries

One of Korčula's minor claims to fame is the existence of an unexpected variety of fauna. It's the only place in the Adriatic where wild jackals dwell. Fortunately, Korčula's jackals keep clear of tourist areas.

The neighbouring island of Mljet harbours a different zoological novelty: a large colony of mongooses. They're descended from a pair imported from India around the turn of the century expressly to eliminate a snake problem.

Now there's a mongoose problem.

---

to make the city one of the Adriatic's outstandingly picturesque ports of call.

The town's geographical bull's-eye and leading architectural achievement is **St. Mark's Cathedral** *(katedrala Svetog Marka),* begun at the outset of the 15th century. During 150 years of construction the style changed from Gothic to 39

Renaissance. Korčula's stone-masons enjoyed widespread fame through the centuries; this church with its ornate portal, eccentric gables and rose window shows why. The interior reveals unusual furnishings and art works of historic interest including an altarpiece by Tintoretto.

Next to the cathedral on the main square, the 14th-century Abbot's Palace has become a small museum of antiquities. The exhibits range from priceless church vestments to contemporary Croatian art.

The municipal museum occupies the Gabriella Palace, a 16th-century mansion across the narrow square.

Another museum adjoining All Saints' church (crkva Svi Sveti), contains a remarkable collection of religious art going back to a 14th-century Madonna.

A final church worth mention: St. Peter's chapel faces the main cathedral; its construction was begun in the 10th or 11th century.

A few streets away, at the elaborately carved main city gate, the town hall evokes memories of Venetian pomp with its stately Renaissance loggias.

For centuries Korčula artists have specialized in statuary.

Also worth seeing are the surviving municipal fortifications, part of a wall which fully enclosed the city until as recently as the mid-19th century.

Altogether the old city contains fewer than 300 buildings, by no means all habitable. Many dilapidated houses have been abandoned since the great plague of the 16th century.

One tall, narrow house—half residence, half museum—is billed as the birthplace of Marco Polo. Although the 14th-century explorer probably never set foot in the house (the dates are topsy turvy), tradition does maintain that he came from Korčula. Regardless of the legend's accuracy, the view from the watchtower of "Marco Polo's house" eases the sting of the admission fee.

Several times each season local talent presents a distinctive folklore extravaganza. The *moreška* is an ancient sword dance clashing in symbolism of good versus evil, Korčula versus the invaders. The costumes, the skill and enthusiasm of the dancers and the potential danger of the sword-play make it an exciting spectacle.

Twenty-one islets surround Korčula. The nearest is Vrnik, known for its stone quarries. Public buildings as far away as Vienna, Istanbul and Stockholm have been constructed of the long-lasting white Vrnik stone.

With traditional pomp, islanders celebrate Catholic holy days.

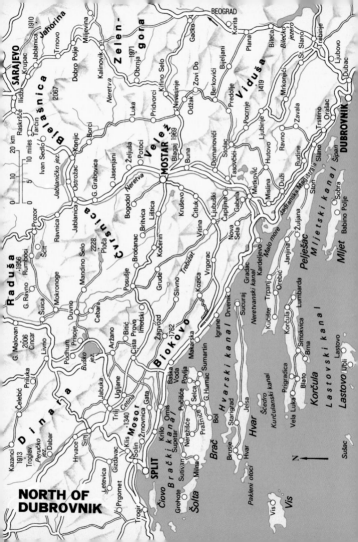

NORTH OF DUBROVNIK

North of Dubrovnik

The enchantment of Dubrovnik extends far beyond the walled city, beginning at the city gate bordering the suburb of PILE. The moody Lovrijenac fortress dominates this scene. It's built into a sheer cliff 150 feet above the sea. During the summer festival, "Hamlet" is performed in this authentic medieval setting.

The parks, villas and hotels of Pile are only the beginning of the northwestward sprawl of Greater Dubrovnik. The chubby peninsula of LAPAD specializes in beaches and resort hotels. Across a narrow bay is GRUŽ—port and shopping area.

Beyond Gruž and its uninviting industrial zone, the Adriatic Highway follows the shore of a long, narrow inlet known as Rijeka Dubrovačka. This area, now largely neglected, was once favoured by weekending nabobs from the Dubrovnik republic. Theoretically the inlet is not so much an Adriatic bay as a narrow underwater valley fed by fresh water from a source at the landward end. Whatever the geographical subtleties, the lay of the land—steep slopes open

to the west wind—encourages less than perfect weather conditions by Dalmatian standards.

Passing through on the way to likelier swimming grounds, you might want to spare some time for the St. Stephen's church *(crkva Svetog Stjepana)*, a Romanesque structure of the 12th and 13th centuries, and a 14th-century Franciscan mon-

---

**The Briny
Not-So-Deep**

The Adriatic is one of the world's more shallow seas, averaging only 57 fathoms (342 feet) in depth. (By contrast, the bottom of the Pacific Ocean reaches 6,000 fathoms in places.)

With a heavy salt content and a scarcity of plankton, the Adriatic is remarkably transparent. You can spot a fish ten yards away. Maximum recorded under-Adriatic visibility: nearly 180 feet.

For centuries the Slavic name for the Adriatic has been Jadran—which explains why so many hotels, restaurants and cafés along the Coast bear that name.

astery. All in all, the ruins of patrician villas, some overrun by the subtropical vegetation, make for a subdued scene.

Nature-lovers will perk up at a beauty spot only 29 kilometres northwest of Dubrovnik, the hamlet of TRSTENO. Between the sea and the unusually fertile mountainside, stone houses radiate from a village square. Here two gargantuan plane trees spread 400-year-old branches; the larger has a circumference of 36 feet. But these specimens are only a

Every turn of the Adriatic Highway opens to spectacular, new vistas.

teaser for the attractions on view at a nearby botanical park. Laid out in Renaissance formality at the beginning of the 16th century, the garden is now run by the Yugoslavian Academy of Sciences and Arts and is known as the Arboretum. Here are some of the star attractions, listed in alphabetical order: bamboo, breadfruit, cactus, camphor, cinnamon, eucalyptus, jasmine, magnolia, oleander and palm trees.

Situated about 15 kilometres beyond Trsteno, the promising tourist area of SLANO exploits a deeply indented bay neatly protected from stormy weather. The clean pebble beaches with calm, clear water lure many vacationers. But the shore here is interesting as well for archaeological reasons with earthworks and graves from the time of the ancient Illyrians. Tourism isn't the only industry in Slano. The local folk specialize in wild herbs. They disperse into the hills to collect laurel, sage, wormwood and other valuable medicinal plants. At the colourful Slano fair every August 2, villagers don traditional dress and dance the *lindjo,* a time-honoured routine not to be confused with the limbo or the lindy-hop.

Continuing on, a side road off to the left leads to the village of STON which lies at the beginning of a 40-mile-long peninsula. Gourmets will be delighted to know that Ston boasts the best and largest oyster beds on the whole Coast. The village's great walls climbing up the stony hillside are reminders of medieval times when it was part of the Dubrovnik republic.

Secluded beaches, crystal-clear water.

Mostar and Sarajevo

With mosques, minarets and oriental bazaars only a few hours away, you won't want to miss seeing the historic city of Mostar. If you've a bit more time to spare you can travel farther inland to Sarajevo, a big city with an exotic cast. Whether you take an organized excursion or go on your own, you'll be impressed at how vastly different is this part of Yugoslavia just beyond the mountains.

On the 130-kilometre trip from Dubrovnik to Mostar an ideal spot to take a break is POČITELJ, a walled town built by the Turks. Over a period of four centuries, they added fortifications, a mosque, a *medresa* (a Moslem theological school), public baths and a clock tower which lost its bell in 1917; the Austrians melted it down to make bullets.

In Počitelj walk uphill to the main mosque (built in 1563). Its shaded terrace commands a pleasing view of the river. A restored Turkish villa nearby houses an artists' colony with an art gallery.

Carrying on toward Mostar, as the highway follows the riv-

er upstream, the valley widens into a dusty plateau. Barely visible against the skyline are inaccessible fortresses. In the midst of this wasteland—an unlikely place for human habitation—you come upon the oriental city of **Mostar.** The minarets of its many mosques reach out above the rooftops. Fanning out from the town are vineyards, groves of fig trees and tobacco fields.

The scene here is dominated by the torrential Neretva River. The ancient arched Turkish **bridge** from which the town got its name (*most* means "bridge") is unforgettable. It was built in 1566 when the town had already been under Turkish rule for almost a century. As the story goes, an earlier attempt to span the river had failed. The sultan vowed to execute the architect if his next bridge didn't stand. The architect Hajruddin stalled as long as he could but when the day finally came to remove the supports he had so little faith in his own project that he fled in fright. He was found later digging his own grave. His pessimism couldn't have been less appropriate. The bridge still stands, a classic of engineering and art.

Not far from the bridge you can see the mosque of Karadjoz Beg, who was the local administrator in the same mid-16th-century era. You may hear one of the five daily calls to prayer—no longer chanted by the *muezzin* from the minaret balcony but over a public-address system.

Here you'll still find some of the men wearing elements of the timeless Moslem costumes: a black-tassled red fez, a red cummerbund (in earlier times holding a pistol or dagger) or pointed leather slippers. You'll see women in billowing Turkish pantaloons but the veil is no longer worn.

As you stroll the narrow street leading to the old bridge, notice that each house is painted differently. This tradition of individualism is carried on in the workshops. Follow the sound of hammering and you'll find an artisan crafting copper, silver or gold into delicate designs. See, too, the woollen carpets in bright geometrical patterns.

Town of Mostar was named after its 16th-century arched bridge.

Moving away from the river you enter what was formerly the commercial centre of Sarajevo, a labyrinth of narrow streets and alleys lined with old, wooden-shuttered booths. Each street is named after the guild of artisans who operated there (Street of the Saddle-makers etc.). Fortunately, it's a pedestrians-only zone.

Close-by is **Gazi Husref Beg's Mosque**, built in 1531, with its bluish-green oriental dome and slender minaret. The courtyard in front contains a fountain and two Turkish mausoleums *(turbe);* the stone turbans inside indicate the rank of the deceased. The mosque itself is carpeted with fabulous Persian rugs presented by Moslem dignitaries, past and present. Sarajevo's first school, a *medresa* built in 1537, and also a red-brick clock tower stand nearby.

Among the buildings that have been restored are the covered market, Brusa Bezistan (1551), and an old Turkish *caravan-serai,* or inn, called the Daire, with rooms opening onto a cobblestone courtyard. Mind your head going in.

After taking a look at the busy market-place, you can return to the riverbank for a rest before going on to further sights. You can climb up to the citadel past lovely Turkish houses with their latticed windows (so women could peer out without being seen). Or if you prefer even greater heights, you can cross the river and take the cable-car up to Mount Trebević for another splendid view.

Leaving Sarajevo you may have time to visit the Regional

In Konavle valley, farmers still till the soil with oxen.

South of Dubrovnik

Museum *(Zemaljski muzej)* for an overall survey of the changing cultures in this area. There are artefacts from the Stone, Bronze and Iron ages, Illyrian and Roman relics and regional ethnographic exhibits: costumes, musical instruments, pottery and household utensils.

Heading southeast from Dubrovnik, the coastal road involves a few moderately hair-raising tests of driving skill and demands caution. The spectacle makes it more than worth the trouble. A memorable sight is the first vista as the road climbs beyond Dubrovnik. As you look back down onto the

walled town, the new perspective confirms the perfection of the city and setting.

Soon after passing the beaches of Dubrovnik's own suburbs, the highway skirts the first of several resort villages on the Bay of Župa. KUPARI, some eight kilometres from Dubrovnik, once manufactured brick and tile. A few kilns can still be found but the in- habitants mostly devote themselves to the burgeoning tourist trade. A long pebble-and-sand beach and several small ones provide the raw materials.

Just down the coast, the village of SREBRENO is protected from northerly winds by its green mountain backdrop. Big modern hotels have staked out the pebbly beaches.

The next village on the Bay

of Župa, MLINI, was named after the mills built where several streams empty into the sea. In addition to the pebble beach, a waterfall and the surrounding cypress and pine groves, Mlini's attractions are as varied as Roman remains, a 15th-century church and a nudist colony.

Another built-up resort, PLAT, is set near an important

hydroelectric plant. However, this overpowering neighbour doesn't disturb the restful air of the beach-front, the stone houses and old church.

The biggest and most interesting tourist centre along this stretch of the Adriatic is **Cavtat** (pronounced TSAV-tat). More than just a pretty beach, this was the ancient city of Epidaurus. When it was overrun by invaders in the seventh century, the survivors founded Dubrovnik.

Unfortunately, few ancient relicts remain. The last of the medieval ramparts fell to eager-beaver city planners in the 19th century. But the seaside setting is hard to beat—a cypress-and-pine-covered peninsula with a stone village of climbing, narrow streets. The parish church, reconstructed in the 18th century, has a slender bell-tower. Next door is a Renaissance palace, now used as a museum and library, with the archives of Baltazar Bogišić, a 19th-century scholar who was a native of Cavtat. Beaches and tourist hotels follow the coastline on each side of the

Setting sail on the sunny Adriatic. 53

⚑ Bay of Kotor

As the Adriatic Highway enters Montenegro we first glimpse the stark, cool beauty of the Bay of Kotor *(Boka Kotorska)*, a world of bold mountains mirrored in a still, blue sea. Bays beyond bays surrounded by oleander, palm and cactus lead up to massive, bare mountaintops. The sea penetrates so far into the mile-high mountain chain that Boka Kotorska has a climate all its own—often stormy.

Not only is this one of the Adriatic's most spectacular natural attractions, it also holds obvious strategic importance. This fjord-like valley has attracted the warships of many nations for thousands of years. It has been occupied by

Greeks, Romans, Ostrogoths, Slavs, Saracens, Croatians, Bosnians, Venetians, Austrians, French, Russians, Turks, Italians and Germans.

The first town to appear as the road winds down towards sea-level is IGALO, once an obscure spa. It has expanded into a busy tourist and ultra-modern medical centre, but mudbaths and mineral waters still attract the hard core of visitors all year round. Nowadays the treatment is called physio-therapeutics.

The main town on this stretch of coast, HERCEG-NOVI, has a long history as a summer and winter resort. The highway stays aloof from the town which is tucked away below and mostly out of sight; the careless tourist might think Herceg-Novi was just another, not particularly distinguished village. Quite the contrary. Elegantly landscaped villas and parks adjoin a quaint old walled city. You enter through an arch supporting a 15th-century clock tower. A 16th-century fortress, called Spanjola, was built by the Turks on the ruins of an old Spanish tower. The Serbian Orthodox monastery of Savina, above the town in a wooded setting, contains two churches of interest. The newer, built in the late 18th century, combines Byzantine and baroque elements. The monastery's treasury boasts exhibits of substantial historical and artistic value including a silver-edged crystal

Left: sea meets mountains in Bay of Kotor. Right: clock-tower gate of Herceg-Novi.

pectoral cross from the 13th century. Along the waterfront, sightseers enjoy the vantage point of a promenade which used to be a narrow-gauge railway line. With the mild climate, the sun and flowers, the spa of Herceg-Novi has not surprisingly multiplied its hotel space to meet the demand.

Yet for the next ten kilometres the coast is undeveloped touristically. The village of KUTI, near the small port of ZELENIKA, boasts the remains of what is thought to be an 11th-century church. And in the next town, BIJELA, aside from its fish cannery and shipyard there's a medieval church with 14th-century frescos.

The bay narrows to a 300-yard channel at the nearby village of VERIGE, meaning chains. In the Middle Ages the inner bay was blocked off to enemy ships by suspending chains across the channel.

KAMENARI is an undistinguished village where a fleet of boats provides an efficient shortcut for travellers too busy to circumnavigate the innermost bay. If you're hurrying to

Peter the Great sent midshipmen to Perast, now a living museum.

Budva or Sveti Stefan, the car-and-bus ferry to Lepetane saves a long and difficult drive. But it would be a pity to miss the sights hidden beyond the straits—some of the most romantic scenery in Europe.

Continuing the long way around by the coastal highway, the first major town, RISAN, was an important outpost of the ancient Illyrian empire. According to Roman war correspondents of the third century B.C., Illyria's Queen Teuta fled to Risan to escape her conquerors. When capture seemed imminent, she took her regal life by plunging into the bay. The Roman connection survives today in some fine 2nd-century mosaics. Otherwise, there are the neat stone houses beneath awesome mountain heights, as well as a park, folklore and archaeological sights which include the remains of ancient edifices now submerged just offshore.

The next town along the coast, **Perast,** has been declared a conservation area, a living museum. This crusty seafarers' port had a shipyard by the 14th century and a naval academy in the 16th. When Peter the Great was founding the Russian fleet at the end of the 17th century, he sent a platoon of his young noblemen to Perast to acquire the necessary know-how. The waterfront, the town square and the streets climbing toward the mountain have a bitter-sweet blend of baroque charm, well-tended flowers and the nostalgia of abandoned mansions. Just offshore are two small islands, SVETI DJORDJE (St. George) with an ancient Benedictine abbey, and GOSPA OD ŠKRPJELA (Our Lady of Škrpjela), an artificial island built by local sailors in the

The ubiquitous array of views, just a kiosk away.

mid-15th century. Its baroque church figures in the waterborne municipal folklore festival every July 22. Nuns show you round the church and its neat little museum.

More shipowners' houses turn up at DOBROTA, a collection of settlements on the northern outskirts of the city of Kotor. Here, beneath a most severe mountain, orange and olive trees prosper, and vineyards sprawl low in the face of chill northerly winds.

Kotor itself is hidden at the remotest, narrowest corner of the most distant bay. Imagine one of those enchanting walled towns with twisting narrow streets and medieval churches —but in a setting which is practically out of this world. Below lies the tranquil sea. Above soars a bare, mile-high mountain. The dramatic layout limits the amount of afternoon sunshine and generally contributes to a rare, moody atmosphere.

Kotor was badly damaged in the 1979 earthquake, but many of the buildings have been lovingly restored, among them the tiny basilica of St. Luke with its Byzantine frescoes, and the Maritime Museum including an interesting section on national costumes.

The city walls were begun more than a thousand years ago under Byzantine rule; the Venetians reconstructed them between the 15th and 18th centuries. At some places the walls were as imposing as a three-storey house—no mean feat considering the era and the steep terrain.

Kotor's seafaring tradition was launched far back in antiquity. The local sailors' guild *(Bokeljska mornarica)* has been in operation since A.D. 809. One legend puts a distinctly maritime slant on the background of the local patron saint. When a freighter loaded

with religious relics from the Middle East took refuge in Kotor, it's said, the residents bought up the most interesting items on board. By chance they pertained to St. Tryphon. St. Tryphon's Cathedral, begun in 1116, was rebuilt over the centuries; the three-aisled basilica is Romanesque with baroque touches. The cathedral treasury is distinguished by an extraordinary silver-gilt bas-relief by the 15th-century Swiss sculptor Hans of Basle, temporarily in the church of St. Mary *(Sveti Marija)*.

But aside from the medieval buildings and museums, this is a city of discovery with unexpected towers, plazas and gates, and perspectives on the eternal collision of the sea and the mountains.

From Kotor the imperative excursion goes to the heart of the old kingdom of Montenegro. This side trip, or more accurately *up*-trip, tackles Mount Lovćen, the 5,738-foot summit of Yugoslavia's smallest republic. There are two ways to go: the traditional serpentine route from Kotor, a thrilling experience for the eyes and the nerves: or the smooth modern highway from

Venetians built stately monuments in strategic city of Kotor.

The goal isn't just mountain-climbing and grandiose panoramas. The end of the line is the storybook capital of **Cetinje**, seat of the Montenegrin kingdom until 1918. Here on a plateau about 2,200 feet above the sea, defended by a wall of mountains, the rulers of Montenegro held court. The great powers of Europe maintained embassies in this obscure redoubt, most of which have been converted into art galleries, museums and libraries. Though scaled down to the size of the kingdom, the official buildings and palaces stir the imagination. The traditional royal palace, for instance, is called the *biljarda* because it contained the only billiard table of the realm—carted up the mountain with excruciating effort. Now it's the home of three museums. Behind the palace, a monastery has existed since the 15th century though it's much rebuilt and modified. The palace of ex-King Nikola (who died in exile in 1921) serves as a museum as well. Cetinje had the first printshop, founded in 1493, in what's today Yugoslavia. Centuries later, type was melted down to manufacture bullets for a war against the Turks in 1853.

Budva. The old road is a startling achievement of late 19th-century engineering, involving 25 hairpin bends in fewer kilometres. It rarely offers the luxury of a retaining wall, or even a symbolic barrier, on the most dangerous curves. In many places the road is barely as wide as two cars. Between mountain terrors, though, you have stirring views of the Bay of Kotor spread out below. For the total Montenegrin experience, go up one way and down the other.

Make a much-needed break at NJEGUŠI, where you might want to try home-made honey-wine, *medovina,* and sheepsmilk cheese, specialities of the region. You can also visit the birthplace of Petar Petrović-Njegoš (see below).

Sightseers survey top of the world from Mount Lovćen.

A worthwhile side trip from Cetinje, now a standard feature of bus tours, climbs nearly to the top of **Mount Lovćen.** There, nature, art and history meet. It's a long haul from the end of the road, up hundreds of wide stone steps which mount the hillside, tunnel through the peak and emerge at what seems the top of the world. This is the highly appropriate spot chosen by a remarkable 19th-century ruler of Montenegro as his burial place.

The **mausoleum** of Petar Petrović-Njegoš—poet, prince, warrior and bishop—reigns over an inspiring panorama of his country and the sea beyond. Translated into several languages, his poetry has left the most indelible mark upon Yugoslavia. The mausoleum was designed by Ivan Meštrović, the versatile Yugoslavian sculptor. Two of his distinctive caryatides, gigantic figures of Montenegrin women, guard the entrance. Inside is a Meštrović statue of Prince Peter in greenish granite nearly 13 feet high. The bearded figure, wearing traditional costume, is shown seated with a book and behind him an eagle symbolizing liberty. The famous Montenegrin, who died in 1851, was both spiritual and temporal ruler of his domain.

The big decision after a visit to Cetinje and the mountaintop memorial is which of three destinations to choose: whether to return to Kotor, to pro- 63 ceed inland to the modern capital of Montenegro, Titograd, or to head southwest over the mountains to the coast at Budva. For reasons of comprehensiveness, our leisurely itinerary doubles back to Kotor in order to continue the long way around the gulf.

On the far side of the inlet beyond Kotor, the only major settlement bears another of these seemingly unpronounceable, nearly vowelless Yugoslavian names—PRČANJ. Try per-CHAni. Here the parish church of the Birth of Our Lady *(crkva Rodjenja Bogorodice)*, the biggest in the area, took well over a century to build. In white marble from the island of Korčula, it offers a 19th-century impression of a Renaissance church.

Just beyond the tip of the Vrmac peninsula we arrive at LEPETANE, destination of the car ferry providing the drastic shortcut of the bay. There are two versions of the derivation of the name of this village. The official story attributes it to the Lepetan family who came from Perast in the 15th century. The unofficial version is much more intriguing. It says Lepetane is a corruption of the Italian *le puttane,* the ladies of the night

who made this a favourite rest-and-recreation centre for sailors of the Middle Ages. Nowadays, though, it's a somnolent, virtuous village.

TIVAT is the second largest city of Boka Kotorska. Most of the 3,000 permanent residents are employed in a shipyard, at the nearby commercial airport or in tourism. In shallow sea just offshore are three islets.

One possesses the remains of a 13th-century Benedictine monastery. Another islet, St. Mark *(Sveti Marko),* has been developed as a holiday resort. Downtown Tivat's municipal park exhibits a cross-section of the area's rich botanical specimens.

Leaving this busy industrial and resort town, the highway goes past salt flats which have been an economic factor here for 2,000 years. Soon the route seems a world away from the sea in the middle of the green Župa Valley on the way to Yugoslavia's southernmost coast.

Dizzying road past Cetinje reveals panorama over inlet of Lake Scutari.

Budva to the Border

The most highly developed part of the Montenegrin littoral begins at BUDVA, a walled town of weather-beaten stone houses. The earthquake of 1979, alas, shattered the place. Hit twice in successive months by the devastating seisms, Budva has risen anew from the rubble; 182 of 287 buildings were either completely destroyed or heavily damaged. Now the medieval flavour is back again—virtually intact. An early tourist, George Bernard Shaw, attempted to describe the town, reminiscent of Dubrovnik in its charm. "Words are inadequate", he sighed. "Even I am left to enjoy it—speechless."

Budva was inhabited since the late Bronze Age. Sophocles mentioned it as a "town of Illyria". Archaeologists discovered fourth century B.C. Greek and Roman remains.

Of the many foreign powers which occupied Budva for better or, usually, worse over the centuries, the Venetians left the most ineradicable traces. They erected the city wall and were responsible for much of the architecture within.

Beyond Budva the beauty of beaches backed by cypress, pine and palm has spurred an untypical rash of tourists. The most enterprising of the coast's custom-built resorts, **Slovenska plaža,** is a sprawling artificial village in white Mediterranean style. It's the last word in mass tourism.

Not so MILOČER, formerly the summer home of the Yugoslavian royal family. Development here has been sternly controlled; the private park of palms and oleander remains a bastion of tranquillity. The royal residence has been converted into a fashionable hotel.

Sveti Stefan, an apparition of beauty next to Miločer, deserves the overexploited adjective "unique". There's simply nothing in the world like this charming, small fortress jutting haughtily out to sea. If anything, it may be too calculatedly precious.

At the beginning of the 15th century, we're told, members of the Paštrović clan settled on Sveti Stefan. It was a small island just off the coast, suitable for fortification to fend off marauding Turks. It was also a likely base for mounting pirate raids on passing ships. Incidentally, the Paštrović community was considered an autonomous district by the area's Venetian rulers.

The island was at first linked to the mainland by a defensive drawbridge. Later a sandbar developed. Nowadays a reinforced walkway serves tourists who approach by the busload. Today's gatekeepers charge admission. Gone are the pirates and fishermen. The fortress is now an island hotel. After the war the whole place was taken over for redevelopment as a resort; its 80 stone houses were gutted and redone as luxury apartments. The delightfully crooked streets seem unchanged from humbler

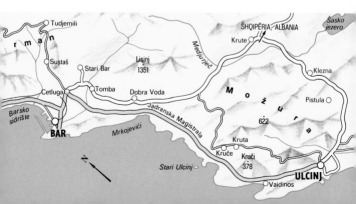

days. There are two small churches worth a look—St. Stephen's, a 15th-century edifice, and the 17th-century Transfiguration church.

On either side of the sandbar is a perfectly curved beach. Non-residents must pay to bathe here.

Much less patrician is the scene at PETROVAC, whose long sandy beach has become the focus of a busy holiday trade. A promenade, cafés and restaurants edge from the front to thick olive groves. A modern pavilion here shelters the area's historical-artistic highlights—a couple of Roman mosaics in multi-coloured local stone. These third- or fourth-century works render imaginative designs on a monumental scale (49 and 121 square feet, respectively).

At Petrovac you can opt for a sidetrip inland to VIRPAZAR and the largest lake in the Balkans. Heron, quail and wild geese enjoy the shallow beauty of **Lake Scutari** (*Skadarsko jezero* in Serbian), which is rich in trout, carp and other fish. The frontier with Albania runs right through the lake, perhaps adding to its sense of mystery.

The next coastal resort area beyond Petrovac sprawls along the wide bay of SUTOMORE. Among the historic sights here is the eighth-century St. Thecla's chapel *(kapela Svete Tekle)*.

Neighbouring BAR, a busy port city, is a transit point for tourists. From here the car ferry crosses to Bari, Italy, and, in the other direction, a railway line goes to Belgrade.

Another world entirely is STARI BAR, a ghost town about four kilometres inland. From afar it looks like a stone relic among the crags of Mount Rumija. City walls of the 15th and 16th centuries delineate a once-prosperous community, deserted nearly a century ago. Among the ruins are a 13th-century cathedral toppled by an explosion in 1881. Another of the doomed city's churches blew up as recently as 1912. Now that the worst is over, the best time to visit is Friday—market day outside the deserted quarter when the local colour brightens the gloom of faded memories.

In Sveti Stefan, the joys of the beach and cultural treasures lie a few yards from each other.

South of Bar a modern highway has eliminated the shocking twists and turns and potholes that used to discourage travellers from pursuing the coast all the way to the Albanian border. The route is not quite one of the wonders of the world, but it stands as a dauntless feat of road-building. It leads to **Ulcinj,** the southernmost and perhaps most striking city on the Montenegrin shore, with vivid splashes of oriental colour.

Donkeys still carry the onions, eggs and homemade brooms to market in Ulcinj,

Sveti Stefan: almost too impeccably beautiful to be real. Right: Children play in forgotten corner of Ulcinj.

led by veiled women in baggy Turkish pantaloons. It doesn't tax the imagination to recall that this town of mosques and minarets was a hotbed of piracy and the slave trade. You may even sight a few local citizens with black skin and African features, descendants of the slaves who got away. And adding to the exotic atmosphere, you'll hear Albanian spoken by a significant proportion of the population.

Ulcinj is said to have been founded thousands of years ago by marauders from the Black Sea. It endured a long series of occupations—by Illyrians, Romans, Byzantines, the Kingdom of Zeta (predecessor of Montenegro), Venetians, the Ottoman empire. And incidentally, Ulcinj wasn't finally an-

nexed to Yugoslavia until as recently as 1920.

The city walls, on a cliff jutting over the sandy harbour, were begun in the 13th century. Not much else is left of the earliest construction because an earthquake in 1444 prompted an almost total urban-renewal program. In the 16th century several hundred pirates were imported from Algeria to make the most of the town's key location on the international trade routes. The pirates and slave traders carried on their commerce until the early 19th century.

Most of the historic buildings were damaged or destroyed in the earthquake of 1979. But Ulcinj has made the most of the disaster, rebuilding spaciously on the ruins. The big new covered market is nearly as exotic as the old, but brighter. Alongside it they've built a modern supermarket; both forms of commerce thrive. Beyond, a cluster of tourist-targeted craft boutiques peddle admirable embroidery and rugs, plus knickknacks of wood, copper and leather.

You might be tempted to join the crowds at the municipal beach in the centre of Ul-

cinj. However, if you prefer powdery sand and plenty of open space you'll be drawn to Velika Plaža ("great beach"), four kilometres east of the town. Velika Plaža is essentially a seven-mile-long beach. It slopes very gradually into a gentle sea, an ideal children's beach. The fine sand is said to be rich in iodine. There's cer-

Take it Off

Naturists—known colloquially as nudists—rate red-carpet treatment in Yugoslavia. Official policy considers naturists to be a wholesome element in the future of world tourism.

The centre of European naturism may be found along the shore of the Istrian peninsula, served by Pula airport. The biggest of these resorts, Koversada, is an entirely naked city with an area of over one square mile.

Along the southern coastline, naturist settlements have been developed at Mlini (near Dubrovnik), on a large scale at Ulcinj (near the Albanian border) and on the island of Ada.

tainly room enough for everybody here. No-one will object if you want to play football, ignite a charcoal fire or blare your radio.

In addition to the hotels in Ulcinj itself, a major tourist zone has been developed along Velika Plaža. Yet the dunes are so endless that the picnickers, castle-builders and nudists can all pursue their pleasures in peace.

The beach goes on to the Albanian border. But don't expect to see barbed wire or sentries or even a warning sign in indecipherable languages. You simply can't get that close... unless you intend to swim it.

Velika Plaža, east of Ulcinj: longest, widest, gentlest beach.

Wining and Dining

If good food is among your weaknesses, Yugoslavia's fresh ingredients, enhanced by recipes from near and far, can meet the challenge.

Along the Adriatic, predictably, the diet tilts toward seafood. But any time you tire of lobster or mackerel you can switch to hearty stews or charcoal-grilled *ćevapčići*, sizzling with the spice of centuries of foreign intrigue. Yugoslavia produces a wide variety of wine to go with every type of dish. Many local wines are first-class; the prices are often beneath their dignity.

Eating out on the coast is delightfully relaxed.

It would be a shame to leave the country without trying some of the exotic and tasty local specialities. This often means venturing beyond the hotel dining-room with its multilingual menus and waiters and "international" cuisine. Leaving our steak or chops diet back home, let's go native and look at some of the new tasty treats in store for us along the Coast.

Where to go? We make no recommendations, award no stars, whisper no tips. Last year's brilliant discovery may deflate into this season's just so-so joint. Even at best, there's no accounting for taste. But we'll tell you what you ought to know before you decide where to dine and what to look for once you're glancing at the bill of fare.

First, how to distinguish the various types of restaurant:

Bife: this is the way the Yugoslavs write *buffet*–a snack-bar where you may order a light, cheap meal, mainly cold cuts, fish, cheese and salads.

Ekspres restoran: a bit short on atmosphere as a rule, it's a rough-and-ready self-service café; limited menu but good for your budget.

Kafana: a coffee shop, often in the Viennese style, strong on rich, creamy pastries and other calorie-crammed snacks; alcoholic drinks also available.

Mlečni restoran: a dairy shop which deals in light meals, pancakes, pastry, yoghurt, milk and even coffee.

Gostiona: a village inn, often privately owned; home-cooked, wholesome food, prepared and served by the proprietor and his family.

Restoran: just about any restaurant from the humble to the elegant.

Riblji restoran: specializing in seafood, but not to the exclusion of meat dishes.

Breakfast isn't a big production in Yugoslavia. In the tourist hotels, bacon-and-egg breakfasts may be obtained but elsewhere it's a matter of coffee, rolls, butter, jam and sweet rolls.

The main meal of the day is lunch though a hefty dinner also figures in the plan. A principal difference between the two meals is that soup for lunch tends to be replaced by a cold first course in the evening.

Meal-times depend on the level of sophistication of the clientele. In fishing villages, for instance, dinner is over early. Elsewhere it could run till 10 or 11 p.m. In hotels, breakfast 75 is served from about 7 to 9, lunch from noon to 2 p.m. and dinner from 7 to 9 p.m.

A service charge, usually 10 per cent, is added to restaurant bills. There are no taxes to be added. If the service was good, leave a tip of about 10 per cent of the bill.

A menu is a *jelovnik*, and here are some of the treats to look for.*

Appetizers

Dalmatinski pršut: Dalmatian smoked ham, a distinctive delicacy of the Coast, justly famous for its subtle flavour.

Gavrilovićeva salama: a tangy salami reminiscent of the best of Italy.

Kajmak: made with the skin of scalded milk, it has a unique flavour and cheesy texture.

Soups

Categorized either as *supa,* a broth, or *čorba* (a thick soup), they come in many varieties and may be grouped together as *juha.*

Festive fiddler reaches for a high note to divert wedding guests.

Brodet: a fish and seafood stew.

Palenta or *kačamak:* maize-meal pudding, similar to what's called cornmeal mush in the American South.

Fish and Seafood

Jastog: boiled lobster, usually served cold with mayonnaise; choose your own, according to size and appearance.

In many restaurants, especially the smaller ones, you'll probably be invited to choose your fish from the refrigerated display case. The usual method of preparation of mackerel, red mullet, bass or similar-sized fish is to grill them over coals. They're served with a strong hint of garlic.

Meat Dishes

Ćevapčići: perhaps the most ubiquitous Yugoslavian dish; they're small sausage-shaped patties of minced meat, grilled and served with chopped raw onion.

Ražnjići: the same idea but consisting of skewered chunks of pork or veal.

Djuveč: as if to prove that there's more to Yugoslavian cooking than kebabs, the Serbs invented this casserole dish of lamb or pork with rice, green

If four languages don't suffice, a picture helps to explain.

pepper, eggplant, carrots, potatoes, cheese and whatever else captures the chef's imagination.

Sogan dolma: a rich Bosnian preparation, generally based on stuffed courgettes (zucchini) and enhanced by a tasty cream sauce.

Sarma: an easy-to-pronounce, homy dish, this is cabbage leaves stuffed with minced meat and rice.

Musaka: layers of minced meat sauce alternating with potato, eggplant or courgettes (zucchini), oven-browned.

Fowl and Game

Piletina (chicken) and *ćuretina* (turkey) are commonly found on menus. During the hunting 77 season you may want to try a more elusive bird such as *jarebica* (partridge) or *fazan* (pheasant).

Salads and Vegetables

Salads most frequently accompany the main dish in both simple and elegant restaurants. A favourite is *Srpska salata* (Serbian salad), a refreshing plate of tomatoes and onion. Another is ***pečene paprike,*** fried green pepper sprinkled with oil. Boiled vegetables also hit the menus in season.

White-smocked cook grills authentic ćevapčići *for outdoor diners.*

Cheese

Each district produces its own cheese, soft or hard, mild or sharp, depending on local taste.

Paški sir: rather sharp, from the island of Pag.

Trapist: the kind the monks produced, made now with regional variations.

Travnički sir: made from sheep's milk, rich and quite salty.

Belava: mild cottage cheese.

Desserts

If you've skimped along the way, you may still be able to contemplate a sweet. The pastries here come under two rich influences, Turkish and Viennese. So if it isn't nuts and poppyseeds, it has to be whipped cream. And sometimes all three. If you have a sweet-tooth you'll rave about the *baklava*, flaky pastry steeped in syrup.

Wines and Beer

From earthy reds to delicate whites, Yugoslavia's wines ought to please almost any taste. Happily, even the best bottles are inexpensive by world standards.

To experiment with local tendencies, order a carafe of house wine. *Bijelo* is white, *ružica,* rosé and *crno* (literally black) means red wine. Mineral water is often served as well; diluting wine in the glass is an optional custom.

Among the better-known wines from the nearby vineyards, these deserve special mention:

Dingač: full-bodied red from the Pelješac peninsula, north-west of Dubrovnik.

Grk: no vowels but plenty of punch in this strong white wine from the island of Korčula.

Žilavka: a more delicate white from neighbouring Hercegovina.

Turkish coffee may not please everyone at first try...

Yugoslavian liqueurs: before or after dinner, or anytime.

Pošip: Dalmatian dry wine, comes in white or red varieties.

Prošek: Dalmatian dessert wine.

If your thirst requires beer instead, Yugoslavian lagers are normally sold only in large bottles. They're much cheaper than imported brands, which come in small bottles.

Other Beverages

Fruit juices are cheap and wholesome. Yugoslavian imitations of foreign soft drinks are less successful while name brands, bottled locally under licence, cost more than some wines.

Tea-drinkers have reported some disappointments. Coffee

is expensive and not necessarily good. If you're accustomed to Turkish coffee, this thick, syrupy liquid is the best bet—though it's not available everywhere. The British Museum reveals that London's first coffee house was opened by a Mr. Pasko from Dubrovnik.

Liquor

Rakija is the generic term embracing all the various liquors you're likely to meet. The locals like a snort before dinner as well as after.

Pre-dinner cocktails, a foreign invention, can be managed in many hotel bars. A Yugoslavian aperitif, milder than most, is *Istra Bitter,* a herb tonic. Imported brands of aperitifs, whiskies and other spirits are expensive.

Šljivovica, plum brandy, is the most famous and popular Yugoslavian liquor.

Lozovača (grape brandy) and *kajsijevača* (apricot brandy) are alternative firewaters, according to your taste.

And don't forget *maraskino,* the liqueur made from maraschino, or morello, cherries.

Finally, *vinjak* is a local brandy reminiscent of a French cognac.

TO HELP YOU ORDER...

Could we have a table? **Možemo li dobiti sto ?**
Do you have a set menu? **Da li imate meni ?**
I'd like a/an/some... **Molim Vas...**

beer	**pivo**	mineral water	**mineralnu vodu**
bread	**kruh [hleb]**	napkin	**salvetu**
coffee	**kafu**	potatoes	**krompir**
cutlery	**pribor za jelo**	rice	**rižu [pirinač]**
dessert	**dezert**	salad	**salatu**
fish	**ribu**	sandwich	**sendvič**
fruit	**voće**	serviette	**salvetu**
glass	**čašu**	soup	**juhu**
ice-cream	**sladoled**	sugar	**šećer**
meat	**meso**	tea	**čaj**
menu	**jelovnik**	(iced) water	**vodu (sa ledom)**
milk	**mleko**	wine	**vino**

...AND READ THE MENU

ananas	pineapple	**file**	fillet
bakalar	codfish	**fileki**	tripe
barbun	red mullet	**gljive**	mushrooms
beli luk	garlic	**govedina**	beef
biber	black pepper	**grašak**	peas
biftek	beefsteak	**grožđe**	grapes
boršč	borscht	**gulaš**	goulash
bracin	bass	**hladno**	cold
breskve	peaches	**hleb**	bread
bubrežnjak	lamb or veal tenderloin	**hobotnica**	octopus
		jabuka	apple
cipoli	mullet	**jagnjetina**	lamb
čaj	tea	**jagode**	strawberries
češnjak	garlic	**jaja**	eggs
čokolada	chocolate	**jastog**	lobster
čorba	soup	**jesetra**	sturgeon
ćufte	meatballs	**kafa**	coffee
ćulbastija	grilled veal or pork	**kajsije**	apricots
		kalamar	squid
dinja	melon	**kavijar**	caviar
divljač	game	**keks**	biscuits
džigerica	liver		(cookies)

81

kobasice	sausages	**prženo**	fried
kompot	stewed fruit	**puter**	butter
kotlet	chops	**puževi**	snails
krastavac	cucumber	**račići**	prawns,
krem	pudding		shrimp
krompir	potatoes	**ragu**	stew
kruh	bread	**rak**	crab
kruška	pear	**riba**	fish
lignje	squid	**riža**	rice
limun	lemon	**saft**	sauce
list	sole	**salama**	salami
losos	salmon	**salata**	salad
lubenica	watermelon	**sardela**	anchovies
luk	onion	**sendvič**	sandwich
maline	raspberries	**sir**	cheese
marelice	apricots	**skampi**	prawns,
maslac	butter		shrimp
masline	olives	**skuše**	mackerel
merlan	whiting	**sladoled**	ice-cream
meso	meat	**smokve**	figs
mladica	river trout	**soft, sos**	sauce
mleko	milk	**svinjetina**	pork
mušule	mussels	**šaran**	carp
na roštilju	grilled	**škembići**	tripe
nar	pomegranates	**školjke**	shellfish
narandža	orange	**škrpina**	scorpion fish
ostrige	oysters	**šnicl(a)**	cutlet
ovčetina	mutton	**štuka**	pike
paprika	green pepper	**šunka**	ham
paradajz	tomatoes	**teletina**	veal
pasulj	beans	**torta**	cake
pečenje	roast	**trešnje**	cherries
pečurke	mushrooms	**tunjevina, tunina**	tunny (tuna)
piletina	chicken	**vešalica**	grilled veal or
pirinač	rice		pork
pivo	beer	**vino**	wine
pljeskavica	hamburger	**voće**	fruit
	steak with	**vrganji**	mushrooms
	onions	**vruće**	hot
pomorandža	orange	**začin**	spice
povrće	vegetables	**zelenje**	vegetables
pršut	smoked	**želudac**	tripe
	ham	**živina**	fowl

82

Enjoy the challenge of shopping in street markets or chic boutiques.

What to Do

Shopping

Buying trinkets from the locals can be one of the memorable features of a foreign holiday. As elsewhere, the Adriatic coast sells a few white elephants among the bargains. One tourist's prize catch is another's dust-catcher.

As for haggling over prices, this is a rare pursuit in Yugoslavia these days. It's almost entirely confined to outdoor markets where craftsmen sell their own work. All the major shops and most of the minor ones belong to unions with fixed prices marked on the goods. It would be futile to haggle in any of these shops and quite possibly offensive. But street pedlars and the owners of small handicraft shops may accept your challenge to negotiate the price.

Even if you've no interest in buying souvenirs, you'll enjoy browsing through the shops for their cross-section of regional crafts. In the non-tourist shops you can see how and what the Yugoslavs buy. Check on local fashions and prices.

In cities and tourist hotels duty-free shops sell a variety of goods at advantageous prices—anything from a carton of cigarettes to a hi-fi system or a nutria coat. Prices are normally listed in German 83 marks (DM), but almost any currency except dinars will do.

Shopping hours follow the typical Mediterranean pattern —early morning to early evening with a long break during the heat of the afternoon. Typically, shops stay open from about 8 a.m. to noon, closing for lunch and siesta and reopening at leisure from 5 to 8 p.m. However, a certain number of shops—mostly supermarkets—remain open all day without a break. These anti-siesta establishments are marked *non-stop*.

Dubrovnik is the undisputed commercial centre of the southern coast, with many handicraft and specialist shops in the heart of the old town, plus modern department stores in the suburbs. However, in smaller resorts as well as the more obscure villages, you may find shops selling items unheard of elsewhere. If you've the time to spare, compare prices city-to-city and shop-to-shop.

Here are some items to look for. Well-travelled visitors consider them either relatively cheap in Yugoslavia or unique —and sometimes both.

Dubrovnik rug merchant's view of the world on a quiet afternoon.

Carpets. Like many handiworks on sale along the Coast, these originate in less sophisticated inland areas; original hand-loomed patterns.

Copper ware, including Turkish-style coffee grinders, pots and cups, exotic and inexpensive.

Crystal. Imaginative and relatively inexpensive, worth keeping an eye out for special pieces.

Dolls. Collectors can stock up on the national costumes of all the republics of Yugoslavia.

Embroidery ranges from handkerchiefs to lavishly decorated skirts and blouses.

Footwear, perhaps made before your eyes, sometimes in the bargain category.

Gramophone records are a bargain—folk-music, the classics or a Balkan version of a pop song.

Lace, like embroidery, is a traditional skill in parts of Yugoslavia.

Leathergoods—luggage, wallets, handbags—need a close look and comparative pricing.

Postage stamps make cheap, thoughtful gifts for collectors on your list.

Posters and prints. Another money-saving idea; look for cheap but good reproductions of charming contemporary Yugoslavian art.

Pottery. For instance, hand-painted plates in bright colours and one-of-a-kind designs.

Spirits. Very inexpensive, often impressively packaged gifts. Consider *maraskino* (morello-cherry flavour) and *šljivovica,* the plum brandy of renown.

Wood carving. Salad sets, statuettes, flutes, knick-nacks, mass-produced by hand.

Woven fabrics. Tablecloths, dress material, shoulder bags, in typical Yugoslavian patterns.

Folklore

Formal or informal folklore performances may be found in several tourist centres. The most extensive line-up brightens the Dubrovnik festival; ensembles from many regions present their traditional songs and dances. In addition, folklore shows are presented twice a week in the medieval Revellin Fort of Dubrovnik.

Every Sunday morning the Konavle Valley folk gather in Čilipi after church for a performance which attracts an audience from miles around. The comely Dalmatian maidens wear red and white pillbox hats, black bolero jackets over loose-sleeved white blouses emblazoned by sun-coloured pom-poms around the neck with hemmed aprons over demure, long white skirts. The women's costumes are made with countless subtle variations denoting age, marital status and other distinctions. Every day of the week the older women are seen in town wearing their stiff, white-winged hats reminiscent of nuns' habits. The men wear red hats like modified fezzes, black waistcoats over loose white blouses and black pantaloons gathered below the knee, revealing long white stockings. They dance to the accompaniment of such uncommon instruments as the *gusle,* a sort of one-stringed violin, and flutes of cane or carved wood.

Farther down the coast, the Montenegrin national costume is even more elaborate: luxurious multi-layered extravagan-

zas in red, turquoise and pale blue. The men, who are very tall, wear swashbuckling outfits with voluminous blue pantaloons tucked into high black-leather boots.

Dangerous dancing is also a famous feature of the island of Korčula, where the Moreska sword dance—derived from an ancient morality play—is performed every July 27 as well as on various occasions during the summer.

Sunday in Ćilipi: Konavle Valley costumes and dances on display.

FESTIVALS

The whole Dalmatian Coast abounds with local celebrations which range from the renowned Dubrovnik Summer Festival to the quaint village fair.

First, Dubrovnik's annual celebration: from July 10 to August 25, something for nearly everyone is staged in the dramatic settings of the old city's fortresses, palaces and squares. Yugoslavian and well-known foreign artists serve up drama, ballet, classical music and folklore. Scores of attractions are organized each season. You can get a detailed programme of events from Yugoslav government tourist offices. If you're serious about the cultural side of your holiday, plan far ahead for tickets and hotel reservations. The area is usually jammed with visitors to this festival which is one of Europe's outstanding artistic events.

The Dubrovnik summer festival has been an annual function since 1950. Another festival, inaugurated several centuries earlier, is held on the first Sunday after the feast day of St. Blaise (Feb. 3), during which relics of the city's patron saint are borne in a candle-light procession through the streets of the town and up the mountainside.

Many other coastal communities observe saints' days or other religious and traditional anniversaries. With luck you may stumble upon a centuries-old ceremony or at least a tourist-oriented carnival. A few samples:

Budva, Sveti Stefan, May 22-27, festival of classical music.

Perast, July 22, sea-borne pilgrimage to 15th-century island shrine; folk music.

Cavtat, August, torchlight processions, fireworks, parade afloat.

Slano, August 2, annual fair with folk dancing.

Kotor, summer, various festivities, "fishermen's nights", regattas etc.; inquire at your hotel or travel office for details.

FILMS

Even the small towns have cinemas. In most places the films are shown outdoors on summer nights; the natural air-conditioning, unlike indoor ventilation, always works. Most of the films are foreign. They're shown with the original soundtrack, be it English, French, Italian or Japanese. Subtitles translate into one of the Yugoslavian languages. Better check with your hotel desk-clerk to determine the language of the soundtrack.

Programmes are not continuous; each showing is a separate sitting. In small towns there are intermissions for changing reels.

NIGHT-LIFE

Up and down the Coast, excitement turns up in unexpected places. A fishing village may be hiding a discotheque as raucous as one could desire. A luxury hotel apparently inhabited only by prim museum-lovers may run a lively night-club—floor show, dancing and all. Some of the bigger hotels have gambling casinos to round out the glamour. Roulette, chemin de fer, blackjack, craps and slot machines compete for your investment. The expertise and equipment have usually been imported from Las Vegas or Reno.

Travel agencies operate night cruises aboard floating dance palaces plying the

Resort night-clubs often stage folklore; here, ritual sword dance.

A bit of tang on nightclub circuit.

Adriatic, with calls at a fishermen's village for more dancing and drinking.

Another travel-agency project, a night barbecue, transports busloads of tourists to a hillside with a view to enjoy the folklore, kebabs and wine under the stars.

The centre of the region's nightlife is Dubrovnik, with its concentration of hotels and nightspots. But the attractions are not only for swingers. The municipal symphony orchestra performs year-round. Other recitals and concerts by local and visiting artists are scheduled throughout the tourist season. All this activity, with drama as well, reaches its peak during the annual summer festival (see page 88).

MUSEUMS AND GALLERIES

Dubrovnik's range of museums and galleries could fill half a holiday. Some highlights:

Rector's Palace, municipal museum including cultural and historical sections.

St. John's Fortress, ethnographic department of municipal museum; maritime museum; aquarium.

Rupe Granary, archaeological collection and folk art.

Bokar Fort, collection of stone fragments from Dubrovnik.

Icon collection, in the parish house of the Serbian Orthodox Church.

Several art galleries, mostly in the old town, display and sell works by contemporary Yugoslavian artists—paintings, sculpture, tapestry and prints. East of the old city, opposite the Excelsior Hotel, a large gallery adjoins a park of sculpture.

Other towns with noteworthy museums:

Cavtat, the Ducal Palace, archaeological and ethnographic exhibits.

Lokrum Island, natural history museum and botanical garden.

Transparent and calm, Adriatic opens a new world to snorkellers.

Herceg-Novi, museum of local history and art.

Perast, museum of local history and art.

Kotor, a collection of historic stones and monuments; maritime museum.

Budva, archaeological-ethnographic museum; also gallery of European and local art.

FOR CHILDREN

All but the smallest tykes ought to enjoy the folklore shows, considering the kaleidoscope of costumes, rhythms and tunes.

Many children are satisfied with the simplest pleasures anywhere—swimming, collecting seashells and intriguing stones and constructing sand-castles. The larger hotels have their own playgrounds and children's paddling pools, table tennis or minigolf.

Boat rides provide an adventurous change of pace—either the local ferries or half-day cruises.

In Dubrovnik itself two outings commend themselves to children with curiosity:

The cable-car sways up to a lookout more than 1,300 feet above the old city—a breathtaking expedition with dazzling panoramas.

And the Dubrovnik aquarium appeals not only to ichthyologists but to any youngster who appreciates the beauty of star-fish, sea-horses and other Adriatic specimens.

91

Walled city of Budva makes romantic background for water-skiing.

Sports and Other Activities

For the vacationer seeking vehement exercise or just a paddle in unpolluted water, the shores of the Adriatic fill the bill for healthful outdoor recreation. Whatever your sport, watch out for too much sun. An hour's excess exposure on opening day is quite enough to spoil everything. Do nothing drastic until your skin has become accustomed to the powerful rays. Wear a hat at midday. You can buy suntan lotion on the spot. Sea urchins and rough rocks make scrambling uncomfortable without plastic sandals.

Swimming is the most basic way of enjoying the placid sea along the southern Yugoslavian coast. Rocky coves, pebbly beaches, man-made embankments and sandy expanses alternate from the Dubrovnik Riviera down to the seaside sahara beyond Ulcinj. Depending on the locale, the facilities may range from zero, or perhaps an elementary shower, to the parasols and pampering bar service on the beaches of luxury hotels.

Snorkelling gives the swimmer an undistorted, uninterrupted view of the undersea world. Sporting-goods shops in the towns sell masks, breathing tubes and flippers but they're expensive. Because of the exceptional transparency of the Adriatic and the proliferation of fish, these are splendid waters for the undersea fan.

Scuba diving is very tightly controlled. You need a permit from the local authorities in charge of internal affairs. Underwater fishing with diving equipment is forbidden. There are zones in which undersea activity is prohibited, such as the area of ports or military installations. Also, large coastal areas northwest of Slano and southeast of Cavtat are off limits.

Boating. If you're visiting Yugoslavia aboard your own yacht, you must apply for a sailing permit at your first port of call. Service facilities may be found in ports big and small. If you'd like to hire a yacht, this, too, can be arranged. A professional crew is optional. At certain beaches you can hire small sailing-boats. Rowing-boats and small motor-boats are also available on an hourly basis.

Water-ski instruction and equipment are provided at beaches between Dubrovnik and Ulcinj. And **para-skiing** is beginning to take off.

A final seaside sport, **fishing;** the number of regulations seems to equal the number of species waiting to take your hook. For the latest instruc-

Sailing's a joy except during bura, *menacing northeast wind.*

tions, check with the local authorities. Equipment may be bought in sporting-goods shops in the towns. Incidentally, after you've gone through any formalities, you may find your daily catch is restricted to five kilograms (11 pounds). Hardly a morning's work, to hear some anglers tell it.

93

SPORTS ASHORE

Tennis isn't a major sport in Yugoslavia but courts do exist at certain hotels as well as tennis clubs.

Golf, however, hasn't come to the area due to the rocky terrain. In the absence of a course of any description, fans will have to make do with **mini-golf,** a common enough diversion around the hotel circuit.

Mountain-climbing begins very near the coast in the Dinaric Alps, which dominate Dalmatia, or Mount Lovćen overlooking Montenegro's shore. Don't underestimate the midday sun at high altitudes.

Hunting expeditions to the interior may be arranged through Yugoslavian travel agencies. There's bear in the hills of Slovenia and Bosnia; closer to the coast, partridge and other wild fowl.

Skiing. In the very early spring, you might be able to alternate between the sunny seaside and the snowy slopes, but it would involve formidable travel. While your coastal resort may back on to a snow-topped mountain, the nearest real ski centre is probably hundreds of miles away. The best-run ski resorts are all in the north, for instance, in Bosnia and Slovenia, which borders on ski-conscious Austria. Package-tour companies run winter sports holidays from Britain to sophisticated Yugoslavian resorts such as Bled and Bohinj.

INDOOR PURSUITS

Bowling alleys have been opened in half a dozen major tourist hotels along the southern coast.

Table-tennis is very widely available.

Chess is more of a major national sport than in most Western countries. If you can play, it's a quick way to meet the Yugoslavs.

SPECTATOR SPORTS

Football. Soccer is a serious pursuit in Yugoslavia though the principal matches are held outside the tourist season. You may stumble onto less formal warm-ups locally.

Water-polo. Each Adriatic village seems to field a team ready to drown for local honour. An exciting game to watch when spirits reach flood tide.

FLORA AND FAUNA

The foothills paralleling the Adriatic in Southern Dalmatia and Montenegro are lush with majestic cypresses and sturdy pines. Maple, oak, ash and elm vary the seasonal tones. In the valleys, gnarled olive trees and vineyards adjoin fragrant almond, peach and orange groves. And all along the coast gardeners pamper the hibiscus, mimosa, magnolia and bougainvillea. Palm, flowering cactus, juniper and heather take care of themselves.

While wild hare, fox and wolves may be occasionally spotted in the hills, hikers interested in the more exotic fauna may quite easily discover bats. They're found in coastal caves, and along the most isolated parts of the shore. Mediterranean seal also survive.

Bird-watchers may not be impressed by the cheerful resident sparrows and finches, but many transient birds are worthy of a second look: warblers, robins and thrushes are present in intriguing categories. Ducks, geese and heron inhabit the valleys.

The Adriatic Sea is home to hundreds of species—enchanting or gruesome, delicious or

Discovering coastal flora is an ideal after-beach activity.

dangerous. Fishermen will often find eel, perch, bass and mullet. The open sea is rich in sardine, mackerel and tunny (tuna). Local menus confirm the proximity of squid, mussels and lobster.

Cautious swimmers will be relieved to learn that, while sharks do appear in the Adriatic, the blue or man-eating monsters are exceedingly rare. For comic relief, dolphins prance capriciously about the local seas.

95

BLUEPRINT for a Perfect Trip

How to Get There

Fares and routes for local and international transport—whether by rail, sea, air, road or a combination of these—are constantly changing. Your travel agent should have the most up-to-date information, but the following outline will give you an idea of the various possibilities.

BY AIR

Scheduled Flights

Direct flights operate to Dubrovnik from certain European cities, mainly in summer. Convenient connecting service is available via Amsterdam and Rome, as well as Belgrade and Zagreb, the main points of entry for transatlantic and intercontinental travellers.

Charter Flights and Package Tours

Charters to the Dubrovnik area operate from various centres in Europa and North America. For those who enjoy sailing, there is a tour combining a week in Dubrovnik with a week of cruising the islands of the Adriatic, Ionian and Aegean seas.

BY CAR

Here are three ways of reaching the area:

1. Drive all the way to the Dalmatian coast, entering Yugoslavia either from northern Italy (near Trieste) or through Austria.

2. Put your car on a train in northern Europe (May to September only). The car-sleeper express, while expensive, saves on fuel, wear and tear and hotel bills. You can take the wheel again at Ljubljana and sightsee refreshed.

3. Drive through Italy and then take a car ferry to Yugoslavia. Ferry-boats link the Italian and Yugoslav coasts at the following points: Venice–Dubrovnik, Ancona–Zadar, Ancona–Dubrovnik, Pescara–Split, Bari–Dubrovnik, Bari–Bar–Dubrovnik, Rijeka–Dubrovnik–Bari and Rijeka–Dubrovnik–Corfu–Igoumenitsa.

The Adriatic Highway, running along the coast, links up with other main roads in Yugoslavia as well as those of neighbouring countries.

By Car Ferry from the U.K. and Ireland: During the summer, be sure you have a firm reservation. Here's how you can go:

1. Via France: Dover–Boulogne/Calais/Dunkirk; Folkstone–Boulogne/Calais; Newhaven–Dieppe; Southampton–Cherbourg/Le Havre; Ramsgate–Dunkirk.

2. Via Belgium: Dover–Ostend/Zeebrugge; Folkestone–Ostend; Felixstowe/Hull–Zeebrugge.

3. Via Holland: Harwich–Hook van Holland; Hull–Rotterdam; Sheerness–Vlissingen.

4. For slightly more than the ferry, you can cross by hovercraft from Dover to Calais (35 minutes) or to Boulogne (39–45 minutes).

BY RAIL

From London and Paris, the Simplon Express goes all the way to Trieste—about a 24-hour ride—and Rijeka. From Ostend, the Tauern Express goes as far as Zagreb and Split. Sleeping and dining cars are available.

Eurailpass: North Americans—in fact, anyone except residents of Europe—can travel on a flat-rate, unlimited mileage ticket valid for first-class rail travel anywhere in western Europe (not in Yugoslavia however—nor in Great Britain). Eurail Youthpass offers second-class travel to anyone under 26. These tickets also give discounts on other forms of transportation. You must buy your pass before leaving home.

Inter-Rail and Rail Europ Senior Cards: The Inter-Rail Card permits 30 days of unlimited rail travel in participating European countries and Morocco to people under 26. In the country of issue, fares are given a 50% discount. Senior citizens can purchase the Rail Europ Senior Card for unlimited travel at a discount.

When to Go

Dubrovnik's climate is generally pleasant throughout the year. Even in February, usually the coldest month, the temperature seldom falls below 42 °F (5.5 °C), and the average maximum temperature for July is 83 °F (29 °C)—as hot as most people like it.

Sea bathing can usually be enjoyed from spring to late autumn, and in the winter many hotels offer heated indoor swimming pools.

		J	F	M	A	M	J	J	A	S	O	N	D
average daily	°F	42	43	47	52	58	65	69	69	64	57	51	46
minimum*	°C	6	6	8	11	14	18	21	21	18	14	10	8
average daily	°F	53	55	58	63	70	78	83	82	77	69	62	56
maximum*	°C	12	13	14	17	21	25	29	28	25	21	17	14
Sea	°F	55	55	55	59	63	72	73	75	72	66	61	57
temperature	°C	13	13	13	15	17	22	23	24	22	19	16	14

*Minimum temperatures are measured just before sunrise, maximum temperatures in the early afternoon.

An A–Z Summary of Practical Information and Facts

Listed after each main entry is its appropriate Serbo-Croatian translation, usually in the singular. You'll find this vocabulary useful when asking for assistance. Because of the linguistic variations you may encounter in different regions, an alternative translation is sometimes indicated in brackets [ ]. If the first expression brings a blank look, try the second.

ACCOMMODATION—see **HOTELS**

AIRPORT *(aerodrom).* The principal airport serving the southern Coast is at Ćilipi, 24 kilometres southeast of Dubrovnik on the Adriatic Highway. Porters are available to carry your bags the short distance to the taxi rank or bus stop. Local buses stop hourly at the airport on coastal runs, but arriving tourists are normally met by airline or travel-agency coaches taking them directly to their hotel in their selected resort town. The modern airport terminal includes a currency-exchange counter, car-rental facilities, travel-agency offices, shops, bars, a terrace and a restaurant.

Check-in deadline for international flights is about 70 minutes before departure.

There is an airport departure tax both for domestic and international flights.

Porter!	**Nosač!**
Taxi!	**Taksi!**
Where's the bus for...?	**Gde je autobus za...?**

ALPHABET. Two different alphabets are used in Yugoslavia. The alphabet you'll mainly see around Dubrovnik is the Roman alphabet, though when you venture into Montenegro, you'll encounter exotic 99

A Cyrillic letters of an alphabet which is very much like the Russian. However, it needn't be a mystery to you. Shown below are the characters which comprise the Cyrillic alphabet, as used in Yugoslavia. The column at left shows the printed capital and small letters, while written letters are given in the centre column. The following column gives the corresponding letters in the Roman alphabet which we're using in this book. At right, you'll find an English word that contains the approximate sound.

Printed		Written		Roman	English
А	а	*A*	*a*	a	car
Б	б	*Б*	*δ*	b	brother
Ц	ц	*Ц*	*ц*	c	cats
Ч	ч	*Ч*	*ч*	č	church
Ћ	ћ	*Ћ*	*ћ*	ć	crunchier
Д	д	*Д*	*д*	d	down
Џ	џ	*Џ*	*џ*	dž	June
Ђ	ђ	*Ђ*	*ђ*	dj or d	seedier
Е	е	*Е*	*е*	e	get
Ф	ф	*Ф*	*ф*	f	father
Г	г	*Г*	*i*	g	go
Х	х	*Х*	*x*	h	house
И	и	*И*	*и*	i	meet
Ј	ј	*Ј*	*ј*	j	yoke
К	к	*К*	*к*	k	key
Л	л	*Л*	*л*	l	lip
Љ	љ	*Љ*	*љ*	lj	failure
М	м	*М*	*м*	m	mouth
Н	н	*Н*	*н*	n	not
Њ	њ	*Њ*	*њ*	nj	onion
О	о	*О*	*о*	o	hot
П	п	*П*	*ū*	p	put
Р	р	*Р*	*р*	r	rope
С	с	*С*	*с*	s	sister
Ш	ш	*Ш*	*ш*	š	ship
Т	т	*Т*	*ū*	t	top
У	у	*У*	*у*	u	boom
В	в	*В*	*в*	v	very
З	з	*З*	*з*	z	zip
Ж	ж	*Ж*	*ж*	ž	pleasure

B **BABYSITTERS** *(beibisiter)*. Babysitting facilities aren't likely to be available on an organized basis. In out-of-the-way spots, somebody's grandmother will probably be recruited. Ask your hotel desk-clerk or at the travel-agency office in your resort.

Can you get us a babysitter for tonight?

Možete li nam naći nekog da čuva decu večeras?

BANKS and CURRENCY-EXCHANGE OFFICES *(banka; menjač-*
nica). In the larger centres, banks are generally open from 8 a.m. to
noon and from 1 to 7 p.m., Monday to Friday, and from 8 a.m.
to noon on Saturdays.

When banks are closed or too far away, you can change money at
identical rates in authorized currency-exchange offices including travel
agencies and hotels. Though currency-exchange offices may close a
few hours for lunch, they usually remain open until early evening.

Try to assess how much dinar cash you will need, because excess
money cannot be reconverted.

I want to change some pounds/ dollars.	**Želim da promenim funte/ dolare.**

BARBER'S—see **HAIRDRESSER'S**

BICYCLES *(bicikl)*. While you can buy two-wheeled vehicles in
Dubrovnik, it's not possible to rent them for getting around on the
coast.

BORDER FORMALITIES. See also CUSTOMS CONTROLS. All travellers
must carry valid passports. Citizens of Great Britain and Ireland may
enter Yugoslavia without visas or formalities. American and Canadian
citizens are automatically given entry visas upon arrival. Of course, if in
doubt about visa formalities, it's wise to check with your travel agent
before you leave home. You're generally entitled to stay in Yugoslavia
for up to 90 days.

No health certificate is required for entry into Yugoslavia.

BOY MEETS GIRL. Attitudes toward life are relaxed along the Adriatic. Except for the southernmost area, with its oriental cast, the flirtation
is comparable to anywhere else in Europe. As in most countries,
however, beware that small towns are much more strict than cities and
tourist-trampled zones. If you haven't made friends on the beach, try the
korzo–the community promenade–at sunset.

BUS SERVICES *(autobuski transport)*. Frequent bus services have
been developed for local and long-distance travel along the Coast. Local
lines along the Dubrovnik Riviera, for instance, operate the most
modern equipment, and the fares are low. However, during the tourist
season the buses can become extremely crowded.

B   Tell the conductor (seated behind a small desk next to the door) where you want to go.

Comfortable express buses link the main localities. You can buy a ticket in advance at a bus station in one of the major towns. To one degree or another, English is usually spoken at information and ticket counters.

When's the next bus to ...?	**Kad ide sledeći autobus za ...?**
single (one way)	**u jednom pravcu**
return (roundtrip)	**povratna karta**

C   **CAMPING** *(kampovanje)*. The concept of a camping holiday is highly developed in Yugoslavia with more than 230 officially recognized sites. Scores of these dot the Adriatic coast, often in prized locations with panoramic views.

Rates depend on the setting and the variety of services available. A local tourist tax is added to all bills.

No special permit is required for camping but you have to use an authorized site. Just pulling up at the side of the road for the night is illegal.

Is there a campsite near here?	**Da li ima kamp u blizini?**
May we camp here?	**Možemo li ovde kampovati?**
We've a tent/caravan (trailer).	**Imamo šator/prikolicu.**
What's the charge ...?	**Koliko košta ...?**
per person	**po osobi**
for a car	**za kola**
for a tent	**za šator**
for a caravan	**za prikolicu**

CAR RENTAL *(rent a kar)*. Half a dozen car-rental firms operate agencies in resorts large and small. If you haven't reserved a car before leaving home, you may be able to organize things through your hotel desk-clerk.

There are innumerable variants in price depending upon the firm involved, the model of car, the length of time you use it and whether you plan to return it to the same place or elsewhere inside Yugoslavia or abroad. The most frequently rented cars are Volkswagen, Renaults, Fiats and Audis. You can rent a Mercedes 220, but it'll cost twice the price of a VW. Chauffeured cars may also be arranged.

A local tax may or may not be included in the rate, but non-deductible collision insurance is always added to the bill.

You must, of course, have a valid driving licence at least one to two years old; the minimum age is generally 21. You must pay a refundable deposit—unless you have an internationally recognized credit card. Depending on which credit card you have, some agencies may offer a 10–20 per cent discount.

Renting a car usually means from 8 a.m. to 8 p.m. Fuel and traffic fines are the customer's responsibility.

I'd like to rent a car tomorrow.	**Hteo bih da rentiram kola.**
for one day/a week	**za jedan dan/jednu nedelju**
Please include full insurance.	**Sa potpunim osiguranjem molim Vas.**

CATERING *(ugostiteljske usluge)*. If you've a holiday villa or apartment and want someone to organize anything from a small reception to a complete dinner, ask the local tourist office for the name of a caterer.

I want to give a... for 10 guests.	**Želeo bih da priredim... za 10 gostiju.**
cocktail party/small dinner party	**koktel/večeru**

CHURCH SERVICES. The religion is predominantly Roman Catholic on the Coast where mass is said daily in the Catholic churches of many cities and towns. In Dubrovnik, for instance, mass is said in the Franciscan church on Sundays and holy days at 7, 9 and 11 a.m. and 7 p.m.; weekdays at 6, 7 and 8 a.m. and 7 p.m.

There's no Protestant church in Dubrovnik.

In Montenegro the predominant religion is Serbian Orthodox. Islam is strongest in Macedonia and Bosnia-Herzegovina.

What time is mass/the service?	**U koliko sati je misa/služba?**
Is it in English?	**Da li je na engleskom jeziku?**

CIGARETTES, CIGARS, TOBACCO *(cigarete, cigare, duvan)*. Yugoslavian cigarettes come in a strong, black Turkish variety as well as in mild blends similar to western European cigarettes. In addition to many local makes, certain American brands are manufactured in Yugoslavia under licence. In larger towns and resorts a few British brands may also be found. As in most countries, the local cigarettes cost only a fraction of the retail price of the imports.

Tobacco shops also sell imported (usually Cuban) cigars and Yugoslavian pipe tobacco, which is highly regarded by connoisseurs.

A packet of cigarettes/matches.	**Kutiju cigareta/šibica.**
filter-tipped	**sa filterom**
without filter	**bez filtera**
light tobacco	**blagi duvan**
dark tobacco	**ljuti duvan**

CLOTHING *(odevanje)*. With its Mediterranean climate, the southern Adriatic coast demands lightweight clothing from June to September—the lighter the better. But on the fringes of the high season—before July and after September 30—you may well need a jacket or sweater for the evening. Although the rainy season comes in winter, you could need a raincoat at any time of year.

Formality in dress is confined to sophisticated night-clubs and casinos. Elsewhere it's a matter of pleasing yourself. That goes for beaches as well; no prudish anti-bikini sentiments here. However, it's reasonable to slip something over your bathing suit for the walk to and from the beach.

Obviously, when visiting churches modest dress is appropriate. And don't forget to wear your comfortable shoes when you go visiting museums or sightseeing.

Will I need a jacket and tie?	**Da li su potrebni žaket i mašna?**
Is it all right if I wear this?	**Mogu li da idem u ovom?**

COMPLAINTS *(žalba)*. Complaint procedures are far less formalized in Yugoslavia than they've become in some other countries.

Hotels and restaurants. See the manager if you're dissatisfied. If this leads nowhere, the local tourist office may suggest further steps.

Bad merchandise. The consumer-oriented society is too new in Yugoslavia to have devised elaborate safeguards. Your best bet here is to return to the shop which sold you the article and appeal to the manager's sense of fair play. If you've got a serious gripe, the *Tržišna inspekcija* (market-control board) in Dubrovnik and other large towns can be of help in sorting things out.

Car repairs. If your car has been badly repaired, or if you believe you've been overcharged, try to settle the problem before paying the bill. If this fails, a local travel office or the *Tržišna inspekcija* may be able to mediate or advise.

CONSULATES–see **EMBASSIES**

CONVERSION TABLES. For tire pressure and fluid measures–see page 109. Yugoslavia uses the metric system.

Length

1 centimetre = 0.39 in. (approx. 2/5 in.)	1 in. = 2.54 cm
1 metre = 39.40 in. (approx. 3 ft., 3 in.)	1 yd. = 91.44 cm
1 kilometre = 0.621 mile (approx. 6/10 mile)	1 mile = 1.61 km

Weight

200 grams = 0.441 lb. (approx. 7 oz.)	¼ lb. = 113.40 g
1 kilogram = 2.205 lbs. (approx. 2 lbs., 3 oz.)	1 lb. = 453.60 g

Temperature

To convert centigrade into Fahrenheit, multiply by 1.8 and add 32. To convert Fahrenheit into centigrade, subtract 32 and divide by 1.8.

COURTESIES. See also BOY MEETS GIRL. Most of the precepts for getting along with people anywhere apply to Yugoslavia–be friendly, be yourself, be reasonable. If the locals put ice-cubes in their drinks and you don't, or vice versa, don't let it keep you awake at night.

Speaking of drinks, if a Yugoslav offers you one, it's just about obligatory to accept. If you're not in the mood for brandy, say yes to coffee. You aren't expected to stand the next round; the hospitality can be returned at a later date. If you're a house guest or otherwise treated to a great deal of food, drink and kindness, you may reciprocate by buying a small gift, preferably for any children in the family. Children are very important in the Yugoslavian scheme of things. (Notice the young couples proudly promenading with their offspring.)

Handshaking, seemingly at every opportunity, is a "must" when greeting almost anybody.

All this old-fashioned central European courtesy (though we're in the Balkans, traces of the centuries of Austrian influence remain) is suddenly forgotten in less-relaxed situations–such as clambering aboard an overcrowded bus. *Izvinite* (excuse me) is about all one can say.

Always ask permission before taking photos of people.

C CREDIT CARDS and TRAVELLERS' CHEQUES *(kreditna karta; putni ček)*

Credit cards: Diner's Club and American Express are the most widely accepted cards. Although many hotels, restaurants and tourist-oriented entreprises accept credit cards, they're by no means known everywhere, particularly in the villages.

Travellers' cheques: These may be changed at banks, hotels and travel agencies and are accepted in many shops and restaurants. You'll almost certainly be asked to show your passport when cashing a cheque.

Do you accept travellers' cheques?	**Da li primate putne čekove?**
Can I pay with this credit card?	**Mogu li da platim kreditnom kartom?**

CRIME and THEFTS *(zločin; kradja)*. In the event of a crime, you may indeed have trouble finding a policeman to assist you. But the nearest travel office or hotel desk should be able to put you in quick touch with the *milicija* (police).

Crime persists under all known social systems, so don't tempt fate by leaving your valuables imprudently unprotected or exposed.

I want to report a theft.	**Želim da prijavim kradju.**

CURRENCY *(valuta)*. The monetary unit of Yugoslavia is the *dinar* (abbreviated *din.*). Sometimes the dinar is referred to as *novi dinar* (new dinar). In conversation, Yugoslavs may refer to *stari dinar* (old dinar), 100 of which make a new dinar.

Coins: 1, 2, 5, 10, 50 and 100 dinars.

Banknotes: 10, 20, 50, 100, 500, 1,000, 5,000 and 20,000 dinars.

CURRENCY EXCHANGE—see BANKS

CURRENCY RESTRICTIONS—see CUSTOMS CONTROLS

CUSTOMS CONTROLS. See also BORDER FORMALITIES. The best policy with customs men anywhere is to tell the truth if they ask any questions; being caught after replying "inexactly" could be embarrassing.

Here's what you can bring into Yugoslavia duty-free:

Cigarettes		Cigars		Tobacco (grams)	Spirits		Wine
200	or	50	or	250 g.	1 l.	and	1 l.

Currency restrictions: While you may bring unlimited sums of foreign currency into Yugoslavia, you may not carry more than 50,000 dinars across the border in either direction, and this amount can only be imported or exported once per calendar year. On subsequent trips, a maximum of 20,000 dinars may be imported or exported.

A note about passports: When you arrive at your hotel, the receptionist will take your passport so it can be registered. It is routinely returned the next morning. In the meantime, there is no cause for concern: the passport, and you, are perfectly safe.

I've nothing to declare.	**Nemam ništa za carinjenje.**
It's for personal use.	**To je za moju ličnu upotrebu.**

DRIVING IN YUGOSLAVIA

Entering Yugoslavia: To bring your car into Yugoslavia you'll need:

- A valid driving licence; an International Driving Licence is recommended but not required
- Car registration papers
- Green Card (international insurance certificate)

The nationality code sticker must be visible at the rear of the car. You must possess a first-aid kit and a red-reflector warning triangle for use in case of breakdown, as well as a spare of bulbs for the head lamps (lights). Seat belts are compulsory.

Motorcycle or scooter drivers as well as passengers must wear helmets.

Driving conditions: Drive on the right and pass on the left; yield right of way to all vehicles coming from the right.

Main roads are being improved but secondary roads can be unexpectedly bumpy. Unforeseen obstructions, such as pedestrians or mules,

D

may catch you off-guard. Be forewarned that quaint local attractions can become perils on the road—horses and carts, donkeys, sheep, goats and old folk who haven't quite adapted to the new age of transportation. When passing through villages, drive with extra care to avoid children darting out of doorways and older folk strolling in the middle of the road, particularly after dark.

Road classification:

Autoput	Motorway/Expressway
Glavni tranzitni put	Main road/Highway
Sporedni put	Secondary road
Lokalni put	Local road

Speed limits: 60 kilometres per hour in town; outside of towns, in the absence of a road sign indicating otherwise, your speed is limited to 80 or 100 kph (120 kph on motorways). A car with a caravan (trailer) mustn't exceed 80 kph, even on the open road.

Traffic police: In summer, in major towns and resorts, the traffic police are easily seen with their white helmets and white uniforms. Off-season they wear blue uniforms. The police patrol on foot, on motorcycles and in cars, but outside of busy town centres they're hardly seen. Reckless or drunken driving may be treated very severely: Yugoslavia has stringent regulations about drinking and driving—allowing only 0.5 per mil alcohol content in the blood instead of 0.8 as in Great Britain and most of Western Europe. For other infractions —such as ignoring a stop sign or breaking speed limits—the driver may be fined on the spot. (On the other hand, the defendant is entitled to demand a court hearing, but this is a time-consuming way to prove a principle.)

Fuel and oil: Fuel available is normal (86 octane), super (98 octane), lead-free (rare) and diesel.

Petrol coupons: These coupons can be bought at travel agencies, at automobile clubs in the country of departure, at the Yugoslav frontier or from an authorized exchange dealer in Yugoslavia, and mean a slight reduction in the petrol prices. Unused coupons are refunded at the border when leaving the country or at the place where they were bought. **NB:** ask your automobile association about the latest regulations, as they are constantly changing.

Note that it is prohibited to enter Yugoslavia with a spare can of petrol in the car.

Fluid measures

litres	imp. gals.	U.S. gals.	litres	imp. gals.	U.S. gals.
5	1.1	1.3	30	6.6	7.8
10	2.2	2.6	35	7.7	9.1
15	3.3	3.9	40	8.8	10.4
20	4.4	5.2	45	9.9	11.7
25	5.5	6.5	50	11.0	13.0

Tire pressure

lb./sq. in.	kg/cm²	lb./sq. in.	kg/cm²
10	0.7	26	1.8
12	0.8	27	1.9
15	1.1	28	2.0
18	1.3	30	2.1
20	1.4	33	2.3
21	1.5	36	2.5
23	1.6	38	2.7
24	1.7	40	2.8

Breakdowns: The Automobile Association of Yugoslavia *(Auto-Moto Savez Jugoslavije, AMSJ)* runs aid and information offices in major towns including Dubrovnik, Budva and Kotor. They're open from 8 a.m. to 8 p.m. You can call on them for help in many towns, usually by dialling 987; rates charged for road and tow services are cheaper than those of garages.

Garages specializing in the repair of the leading makes of cars are found only in the larger cities. Privately run garages elsewhere can probably tide you over with ingenious stop-gap methods. But insist on a realistic price estimate in advance. If you need replacement parts there may be a problem of long delays. Spare parts are readily available for cars assembled in Yugoslavia: Citroën, Fiat, Renault, Volkswagen and the Zastava 101. The automobile association can help with urgent shipments. Naturally, an ounce of prevention—a thorough check of your car before you ever leave home—can avoid many a holiday headache on the road.

D **Parking:** In larger towns parking meters now monitor the inactive hours of visiting vehicles. Car parks have also been introduced, sometimes using parking meters.

Incidentally, wherever you park–in towns or on a country road–the law requires that you park your car in the direction of moving traffic, on the right-hand side, never facing the flow of traffic. If you leave your car in a no-parking zone it may be towed away.

Road signs: The standard international picture-signs are in general use throughout Yugoslavia. But here are a few of the more common written notices you may encounter:

Aerodrom	Airport
Automehaničar	Car mechanic
Centar grada	Town centre
Garaža	Garage
Milicija	Police
Odron kamenja	Falling rocks
Opasna krivina	Dangerous curve
Opasnost	Danger
Radovi na putu	Road works (Men working)
Stoj	Stop
Škola	School
Uspon	Steep hill

(International) Driving Licence	**(medjunarodna) vozačka dozvola**
Car registration papers	**saobraćajna dozvola**
Green Card	**zelena karta**

Are we on the right road for ... ?	**Da li je ovo put za... ?**
Full tank please, top grade.	**Napunite molim Vas, super.**
Check the oil/tires/battery.	**Proverite ulje/gume/akumulator.**
I've had a breakdown.	**Kola su mi u kvaru.**
There's been an accident.	**Dogodio se nesrećni slučaj.**

DRUGS. The authorities take a very dim view of anyone choosing Yugoslavia as a corridor for drug smuggling.

DRY-CLEANING–see **LAUNDRY**

E **ELECTRIC CURRENT** *(električna struja).* The standard voltage in Yugoslavia is 220 volt, 50 cycle A.C. American appliances will need transformers and plug adapters.

If your hair-dryer or other electric appliance breaks down, ask your hotel desk-clerk if he can recommend an electrical repair shop or local handyman to rescue you.

I'd like an adaptor/ a battery.	**Želim adaptor/ bateriju.**

EMBASSIES *(ambasada)*

British Embassy*: Generala Ždanova 46, Belgrade; tel. 645-055

Canadian Embassy: Proleterskih brigada 69, Belgrade; tel. 434-524

U.S. Embassy: Kneza Miloša 50, Belgrade; tel. 645-621

Where's the British/American Embassy? It's very urgent.	**Gde je Britanska/Američka ambasada ? Veoma je hitno.**

* also for citizens of Commonwealth countries

EMERGENCIES. Depending on the nature of the emergency, refer to the separate entries in this section such as EMBASSIES, MEDICAL CARE, POLICE etc. If there's no time, put your problem into the hands of your hotel desk-clerk, travel agency or a taxi driver.

Though we hope you'll never need them, here are a few key words you might like to learn as insurance:

Careful	**Oprezno**	Police	**Milicija**
Fire	**Vatra**	Stop	**Stanite**
Help	**U pomoć**	Stop thief	**Držite lopova**

FIRE. Forest fires are a real menace in summer so be very careful where you throw your cigarette butts and matches. Note that some zones—clearly marked—prohibit both smoking and open fires. If you're enjoying a legal campfire, don't forget to extinguish it and douse it with water before leaving.

GUIDES and INTERPRETERS *(vodič; tumač).* The average tourist won't need any special assistance. Hotel personnel can deal with most linguistic problems, and the travel agencies provide competent multi-lingual guides to conduct their tours.

G   However, if you need personalized interpreting or guidance for business or pleasure, apply to one of the travel agencies in the nearest city or resort.

We'd like an English-speaking guide.	**Hteli bismo engleskog vodiča.**
I need an English interpreter.	**Trebam tumača za engleski jezik.**

H   **HAGGLING** *(cenkanje)*. Almost without exception shops in Yugoslavia post their prices and stick by them; haggling might be considered offensive. But if you're shopping for souvenirs at outdoor bazaars or from pushcart-pedlars, by all means try to negotiate a better price.

HAIRDRESSER'S and BEAUTY SALONS *(frizer ; kozmetički salon)*. Prices are more than double if you patronize the salons in luxury hotels rather than neighbourhood shops.

Tip about 10 per cent.

haircut	**šišanje**
shave	**brijanje**
shampoo and set	**pranje kose i češljanje**
permanent wave	**trajna ondulacija**
colour chart	**pregled boja**
colour rinse	**preliv**
manicure	**manikir**
Don't cut it too short.	**Nemojte suviše visoko.**
A little more off (here).	**Odrežite još malo (ovde).**
How much do I owe you?	**Koliko sam dužan?**

HEALTH. Most tourists who suffer health problems in Yugoslavia have only themselves to blame–for overdoing the sunshine and inexpensive alcohol. If you want to protect a delicate stomach, take it easy on the adventurous foods for the first few days and stick to the excellent mineral waters.

HITCH-HIKING *(autostop)*. It's permitted but it isn't always carefree. Traffic is relatively light, and a high percentage of passing cars are loaded with passengers and luggage.

112 Can you give us a lift to…?	**Možete li nas povesti do…?**

HOTELS and ACCOMMODATION *(hotel; smeštaj)*. Hotels in Yugoslavia are officially graded in five categories. "L" is deluxe and from there the classifications descend from A to D, the latter being the lowest grade which earns the title hotel. The classifications are designed to give you an idea of what facilities are offered and what they should cost.

Luxury hotels, extremely rare, measure up to the highest international standards. Full board in a Luxury hotel may cost twice as much as the room rate in a slightly less elegant A-class hotel. Unless half or full board is part of the room rate, breakfast isn't generally included.

The rates are considerably reduced during off-season. Also, for long stays you can normally get a reduction on the daily rate. A tourist tax is charged to every traveller whether he stays in a hotel or is camping. The tax, depending upon the season and local regulations, is added to the bill.

Other forms of accommodation:

A **pansion** (boarding house) has fewer facilities than a hotel. They're graded in three categories: I to III.

A **turističko naselje** ("tourist village") may consist of bungalows or pavilions sprawling around a central core of restaurants and public rooms.

A **motel** (motel), a recent innovation along Yugoslav highways, is sometimes tied in with car-repair facilities.

A **stan** or **vila** (apartment/villa) is a popular holiday accommodation for many tourists to Yugoslavia but may be difficult to arrange at the last moment. Write to inquire at the tourist office of the resort of your choice.

Soba (room); in popular resorts rooms in private homes often outnumber hotel rooms. They're closely supervised and graded (from I to IV) according to the degree of comfort provided. Accommodation can be arranged through the local tourist office. Landladies canvassing near ferry and bus terminals pester arriving tourists.

Whether all your problems have been solved far in advance by a package-tour operator, or you arrive without any warning, housing can certainly be arranged. However, at the height of the season the unexpected visitor may have to settle for an extremely modest roof over his head.

a double/single room	**soba sa dva kreveta/sa jednim krevetom**
with/without bath	**sa kupatilom/bez kupatila**
What's the rate per night?	**Koliko staje za jednu noć?**

H **HOURS** (see also Banks and Post Offices)

Consulates/Embassies are usually open from 8 or 8.30 a.m. to 12.30 or 1 p.m. and reopen between 1.30—3.30 to 5 p.m., Monday to Friday (some close in the afternoon on certain weekdays).

Offices: 7 a.m. to 2 or 3 p.m., Monday to Friday.

Shops: 8 a.m. to noon and 5 to 8 p.m., Monday to Friday, 8 a.m. to 2 or 3 on Saturdays. Most self-service shops, department stores and food shops, however, are open non-stop.

I **INTERPRETERS**–see **GUIDES**

L **LANGUAGE.** Few countries can claim a more confusing linguistic situation. In Yugoslavia there are three major languages with equal status and two alphabets: the Latin one to which we're accustomed and the Cyrillic, similar to Russian.

All along the Dalmatian Coast as far as the Bay of Kotor the language is Serbo-Croatian, which is spoken in most of the country. Beyond the bay, in Montenegro, though the basic language remains, the alphabet changes. Yugoslavia's other two languages are Slovenian (spoken in the northwest) and Macedonian (spoken in the southeast). These three languages closely resemble one another. (Other languages–Albanian, Bulgarian, German, Hungarian, Romanian, Slovak and Turkish–are used by minorities in distinct regions of the nation.)

Nowadays German and Italian are the most widely understood foreign languages along the Coast with English not too far behind. On a brief visit to Yugoslavia the most useful tool is Serbo-Croatian, understood by practically everyone in the country. A few words of that language–or Macedonian, if you're visiting that region–will go a long way towards producing a smile and friendship.

	Serbo-Croatian	Macedonian
Good morning	*Dobro jutro*	*Dobro utro*
Good afternoon	*Dobar dan*	*Dobar den*
Good evening	*Dobro veče*	*Dobro veče*
Thank you	*Hvala*	*Blagodaram*
You're welcome	*Nema na čemu*	*Ništo*
Please	*Molim*	*Molam*
Goodbye	*Zbogom*	*Dogledanje*

The Berlitz phrase book, SERBO-CROATIAN FOR TRAVELLERS, covers almost all situations you're likely to encounter in your travels in Yugoslavia.

Does anybody here speak English?   **Da li neko ovde govori engleski?**

LAUNDRY and DRY-CLEANING *(pranje rublja; hemijsko čišćenje)*.
Most hotels will handle your laundry and dry-cleaning relatively swiftly. Otherwise, you can go to a local laundry or dry-cleaner's, which in any case will be cheaper.

I want these clothes ...	**Želim ove stvari da se ...**
cleaned	**očiste**
washed	**operu**
ironed	**ispeglaju**

When will it be ready?	**Kada će biti gotovo?**
I must have this for tomorrow morning.	**Ovo mi treba za sutra ujutro.**

LAWYERS and LEGAL SERVICES *(advokat; pravna usluga)*. In case of serious trouble, ask your embassy for advice.
If your problem stems from a road mishap and you're a member of a motoring or touring association at home, free legal advice may be obtained from the Automobile Association of Yugoslavia.

LOST AND FOUND PROPERTY; LOST CHILDREN *(biro za nadjene stvari; izgubljeno dete)*. Inquire first at your hotel desk or the nearest tourist office. Then report the loss to the *milicija* (police).
As for lost children, hotel personnel are accustomed to these crises and will help with sympathy and knowledgeable action.

I've lost my wallet.	**Izgubio sam novčanik [lisnicu].**
I've lost my handbag.	**Izgubila sam tašnu.**

MAIL *(pošta)*. If you're uncertain of your holiday address, you may have letters sent to you, care of poste restante (general delivery) at the local post office. Mail should be addressed as follows:

> Mr. John Smith
> Post Restant
> Cavtat
> Yugoslavia

In large cities where there's more than one post office, mail may be picked up at the town's main post office.

When you claim your mail you'll have to produce your passport as identification.

Note: Dubrovnik's main post office at 22, Put Maršala Tita is open for *post restant* retrievals daily from 7 a.m. to 9 p.m. In smaller towns the hours are considerably shorter.

MAPS *(plan [karta])*. Yugoslav National Tourist Offices in your country issue free maps pinpointing resort areas.

On the spot, bookshops along the Coast sell maps with greater detail. For the most serious explorers, the Yugoslav Lexicographical Institute has produced *The Yugoslav Coast, Guide and Atlas*. This impressively researched book contains listings for hundreds of towns and villages, plus 27 maps.

a street plan of...	**plan grada...**
a road map of this region	**plan [karta] cesta toga kraja**

MEDICAL CARE *(lekarska usluga)*. See also HEALTH and EMERGENCIES. Citizens of half a dozen western European countries—including Great Britain—are entitled to free medical care under reciprocal agreements with Yugoslavia. Citizens of other countries must pay for medical services.

For help in minor emergencies look for an *apoteka* or *ljekarna* (chemist's or drugstore) or an *ambulanta* (first-aid post) displaying a red cross.

Pharmacies. In an *apoteka* you'll find both non-prescription medicines and those made up according to a prescription. In a *drogerija* you'll find a great range of toilet articles, cosmetics and the like, sometimes films, too.

In the window of an *apoteka* you'll see a notice telling you where the nearest all-night chemist is. In larger towns, some chemists are open day and night. Their names and addresses can be found in daily newspapers.

If you're required to take certain medicine regularly, it would be wise to stock up before you leave home. Specific brands of medicine might not always be available locally in Yugoslavia.

a doctor	**doktor [lekar]**
an ambulance	**kola za hitnu pomoć**
hospital	**bolnica**
an upset stomach	**pokvaren stomak**
sunstroke	**sunčanica**
a fever	**groznica**

NEWSPAPERS and MAGAZINES *(novine; časopis)*. Most leading western European newspapers, including British dailies and the American *International Herald Tribune* published in Paris, are sold at all major resorts. The papers usually arrive the day after publication. Popular foreign magazines are also sold at the same shops or stands.

Have you any English-language newspapers?	**Imate li novine na engleskom ?**

PETS and VETS *(ljubimci-životinje; veterinar)*. Though *you* may not need a visa to enter Yugoslavia, your dog or cat won't be allowed across the border without a veterinary certificate. This must attest to the animal's good health, include a vaccination record and affirm that you'll submit the pet to an examination by a Yugoslav vet at the border.

In many resort areas, if you need a vet you may find he's more attuned to the needs of mules and goats than chihuahuas.

Returning to Great Britain or Eire, your pet will have to undergo six months of quarantine. Both the U.S. and Canada reserve the right to impose quarantine.

PHOTOGRAPHY *(fotografisanje)*. You can buy film everywhere in Yugoslavia but to be sure of having your favourite brand, and to save on cost, bring your own supply from home (see CUSTOMS CONTROLS, page 107). Photo shops in cities and even small towns advertise speedy developing. For colour film, though, it's probably faster to take your exposed film back home with you for development.

Certain areas—generally near military installations and national borders—are off limits to photographers. They're clearly marked with signs depicting an old-fashioned bellows camera crossed out with a diagonal red line.

The quaintly costumed people you may come across are usually quite accustomed to cameras. However, if you detect any embarrassment or annoyance, the decent course is to desist. One snapshot is scarcely worth an international incident. And less shy subjects are probably ready to be filmed around the next bend in the road.

Beware of lighting situations you might not have encountered before—especially the blinding reflections from the sea and white buildings. You may not be able to rely on the electric eye on your automatic camera in these situations. The secret is to compensate for the reflections with a faster shutter speed. Read your instruction book carefully or, before leaving home, talk over the problem with your camera dealer.

I'd like a film for this camera.	**Želim film za ovu kameru.**
a black-and-white film	**crno-beli film**
a colour film	**u boji [kolor] film**
a colour-slide film	**film za kolor dijapozitive**
35-mm film	**trideset pet milimetara film**
super-8	**super osam**
How long will it take to develop (and print) this?	**Koliko vremena treba da se razvije film (i izrade fotografije)?**

POLICE *(milicija)*. The national police, wearing blue uniforms and armed, maintain public order and control traffic. Each policeman's identity is revealed by his service number, clearly engraved on his belt buckle. If you have any complaints, just remember to look the law in the belly.

Where's the nearest police station?	**Gde je najbliža milicijska stanica?**

POST OFFICE and TELEGRAMS *(pošta; telegram)*. The main post office in Dubrovnik (Put Maršala Tita 22, in Pile) is open from 7 a.m. to 10 p.m. without a break though some sections have shorter hours. (Some post offices limit acceptance of registered mail to certain times; see posted hours.) Besides mail, this office accepts telegrams as well as long-distance telephone calls (see also TELEPHONE).

In smaller towns the post offices operate on reduced schedules, for instance from 8 a.m. to 1 p.m. and from 5 to 8 p.m.

You can buy your stamps at tobacconists' as well.

Airmail is recommended to all destinations unless time isn't essential. Registered letters and packages must be presented unsealed; the postal clerk will seal them in your presence.

Mailboxes in Yugoslavia, painted yellow, are usually affixed to house walls.

Telegrams: There's 24-hour telegram service in Dubrovnik.

express (special delivery)	**ekspres**
airmail	**avionom**
registered	**preporučeno**
poste restante (general delivery)	**post restant**
A stamp for this letter/postcard, please.	**Molim Vas marku za ovo pismo/ za ovu kartu.**
I want to send a telegram to...	**Želim da pošaljem telegram za...**

PRICES. Inflation in Yugoslavia rages so fiercely that prudent merchants write their price tags in pencil. And the dinar dwindles against foreign currencies almost as fast as the bankers can fix the charts in their windows. Thus the following typical price are the merest approximation, and expressed in the less volatile terms of U.S. dollars or German marks.

Camping. $3.50 per person per night, $1.30 for tent or car, $2 per caravan (trailer).

Car hire. *Renault 4* $17 per day, 17¢ per km., $281 per week with unlimited mileage. *VW Golf* $31 per day, 31¢ per km., $511 per week with unlimited mileage. *Opel Kadett* $48 per day, 48¢ per km., $789 weekly unlimited mileage. Add 15% tax.

Entertainment. Discotheque DM 1.50, cinema DM 1, symphony concert DM 3-6.50, folklore performance DM 3-6.50.

Hairdressers. *Woman's* shampoo and blow-dry DM 10.50, permanent wave DM 10.50. *Man's* haircut DM 2.

Hotels (double room with breakfast). De luxe $60-130, Class A $32-100, Class B $19-58, Class C $16-44.

Meals and drinks. Lunch/dinner (fairly good establishment) DM 20, coffee DM 1. Yugoslav brandy and most Yugoslav drinks DM 1.50, litre of local wine DM 6-8, soft drinks DM 1.50.

Is there an admission charge?	**Koliko staje ulaz?**
Have you something cheaper?	**Imate li nešto jevtinije?**
How much?	**Koliko staje?**
It's too much.	**Suviše je skupo.**

P PUBLIC HOLIDAYS *(državni praznik)*

Jan. 1, 2	*Nova godina*	New Year
May 1, 2	*Prvi maj*	Labour Days
July 4	*Dan borca*	Veterans' Day
Nov. 29, 30	*Dan Republike*	Republic Days

In addition, a Day of the Uprising *(Dan Ustanka)* is celebrated on July 27 in Croatia and on July 13 in Montenegro.

Are you open tomorrow? **Da li je otvoreno sutra?**

R RADIO and TV *(radio; televizija)*. Two Yugoslav television channels serve the area. Feature films are usually shown with the original sound-track and subtitles. You don't have to understand Serbo-Croatian to follow sports or musical shows.

On medium-wave radio, the local programmes of a good many European countries are easily picked up on any transistor. BBC and Voice of America programmes are heard most clearly on short wave in the early morning and at night.

S SCOOTERS–see **BICYCLES**

SEAMSTRESSES and TAILORS *(krojačica; krojač)*. If your clothing suddenly needs minor alterations, ask your hotel maid or desk-clerk to send it out for repairs. If you're more adventurous—or desperate—take the problem to the nearest town. There's no shortage of tailors; you can see them sewing in their ground-floor workrooms facing the street.

Could you mend this by **Možete li popraviti ovo do sutra**
tomorrow evening? **uveče?**

SHOE-SHINES *(čišćenje cipela)*. Except for the occasional itinerant shoeshine boy working the open-air cafés, your best bet is a shoe repair stand.

TAXIS *(taksi)*. Clearly marked taxis are available at ranks in all towns and tourist centres, but tend to be rather expensive. Taxis in larger towns have meters, but in smaller places, where there may be only one taxi, ask about the fare in advance. Extra charges are levied for luggage and night travel.

TELEGRAMS–see **POST OFFICES**

TELEPHONE *(telefon)*. Most towns have telephones on the street from which you may dial local calls by depositing 2 dinars.

For long-distance calls, the telephone office is located in the local post office. In most localities in Yugoslavia, you can dial direct to western Europe. Or, if you prefer, your hotel switchboard should be able to handle any calls, local or international.

If you're having difficulty spelling names, use this foolproof Yugoslavian telephone alphabet:

A	Avala	F	Foča	N	Niš	V	Valjevo
B	Beograd	G	Gorica	Nj	Njegoš	Z	Zagreb
C	Cetinje	H	Hercegovina	O	Osijek	Ž	Žirovnica
Č	Čačak	I	Istra	P	Pirot		
Ć	Ćuprija	J	Jadran	R	Rijeka		
D	Dubrovnik	K	Kosovo	S	Skopje	Q	Kvadrat
Dj	Djakovo	L	Lika	Š	Šibenik	W	Duplo V
Dž	Džamija	Lj	Ljubljana	T	Titograd	Y	Ipsilon
E	Evropa	M	Mostar	U	Uroševac	X	Iks

Some useful numbers:

Police	92	Telegrams	96
Fire	93	Inquiries	988
Ambulance	94	General information	981

May I use your telephone?	**Mogu li se poslužiti Vašim telefonom?**

TIME DIFFERENCES. Yugoslavia sticks to Central European Time (GMT + 1) as does most of the Continent. In summer, the clock is put one hour ahead (GMT + 2).

Los Angeles	Chicago	New York	London	**Dubrovnik**
11 a.m.	1 p.m.	2 p.m.	7 p.m.	**8 p.m.**

TIPPING. Hotel bills are all-inclusive. Though restaurant bills feature a 10 per cent service charge, it is usual to tip the waiter 5 to 10 per cent.

Further recommendations (in U.S. dollars):

Barber/Hairdresser	10%
Lavatory attendant	$0.25
Maid, per week	$3
Hotel porter, per bag	$0.50
Taxi driver	optional
Tour guide	5–10%
Bus driver on excursions	$0.50

TOILETS. Though public conveniences aren't very widely distributed or advertised, you need look no farther than the nearest hotel, restaurant or bar.

The facilities are usually marked by symbols rather than words (*muški* for men and *ženski* for women).

The symbols are either a silhouette of a flat shoe for men and a high-heeled shoe for women or the more conventional stick figures of a man or a woman.

Where are the toilets?   **Gde je VC** (pronounced *ve-tse*)
                                molim Vas?

TOURIST INFORMATION OFFICES (*turistički biro*). In major cities of Europe and America, Yugoslav National Tourist Offices offer complete information to help you plan your holiday. They'll also let you consult a copy of the master directory of hotels in Yugoslavia, listing all facilities and rates. Among the addresses:

British Isles: 143, Regent St., London W.1.; tel. (01) 734-5243

122 **U.S.A.:** 630 5th Ave., New York, N.Y. 10022; tel. (212) 757-2801

The offices can supply maps, leaflets and brochures on general or specialized subjects about Yugoslavia.

Once on the spot you'll find municipal tourist information offices in virtually all of the major resorts. In the old quarter of Dubrovnik, a tourist information centre is maintained at 1, Placa, telephone 26-354. For information and help in English between 5 a.m. and 9 p.m., dial 011-980.

Travel-agency offices also stand ready to answer your questions. Some of the agencies you'll encounter in Adriatic resorts are Atlas, Centroturist, Dalmacijaturist, Generalturist, Kompas, Putnik and Yugotours.

Where's the tourist office?	**Gde je turistički biro?**

TRAINS *(vlak [voz])*. A railway links Belgrade to the Montenegrin shore at Bar. Along the southern coast, travel by bus is highly developed, inexpensive and practical. But the main railway lines elsewhere in Yugoslavia are served by modern, comfortable trains. You may book first- or second-class accommodation; you save about one-fourth in second class. The priority and speed of the train is indicated by its category—local, intercity express or international express. In season, trains tend to be crowded and slow; it's wise to book seats and sleeping accommodation in advance—and don't be in a rush.

TRAVELLERS' CHEQUES—see **CREDIT CARDS**

WATER *(voda)*. You may quaff with confidence from a medieval fountain or the carafe on your café table. But while the drink is safe, the change in mineral content in any unaccustomed water may disturb delicate stomachs. If you're sensitive, stick to bottled mineral water (*mineralna voda* or *kisela voda*). It's inexpensive and tasty.

a bottle of mineral water	**flaša mineralne vode**
carbonated	**gazirane**
non-carbonated	**ne gazirane**
Is this drinking water?	**Da li je ovo voda za piće?**

Y **YOUTH and STUDENT HOSTELS** *(omladinski dom; studentski dom)*. Organized holidays and travel for young people are co-ordinated by the Bureau for the International Exchange of Youth and Students, at Moše Pijade 12, Belgrade. This entity operates two large youth centres along the southern Coast in Dubrovnik and Bečići near Budva.

For a less organized way of life, young tourists may live economically on camping sites and in rented rooms in private homes.

Can I hire/buy a sleeping bag?	**Mogu li unajmiti/kupiti vreću za spavanje?**

SOME USEFUL EXPRESSIONS

yes/no	**da/ne**
please/thank you	**molim/hvala**
excuse me/you're welcome	**izvinite/molim**
where/when/how	**gde/kad/kako**
how long/how far	**koliko dugo/koliko daleko**
yesterday/today/tomorrow	**juče/danas/sutra**
day/week/month/year	**dan/nedelja/mesec/godina**
left/right	**levo/desno**
up/down	**gore/dole**
good/bad	**dobro/loše**
big/small	**veliko/malo**
cheap/expensive	**jeftino/skupo**
hot/cold	**vruće/hladno**
old/new	**staro/novo**
open/closed	**otvoreno/zatvoreno**
Where are the toilets?	**Gde su toaleti?**
Waiter!/Waitress!	**Konobar!/Konobarica!**
I'd like…	**Želeo bih…**
How much is that?	**Koliko staje?**
What time is it?	**Koliko je sati?**
What does this mean?	**Šta ovo znači?**
Is there anyone here who speaks English?	**Da li ima neko ko govori engleski?**
I don't understand.	**Ne razumem.**
Please write it down.	**Molim Vas napišite mi to.**

124

DAYS OF THE WEEK

Sunday	nedelja	Thursday	četvrtak
Monday	ponedeljak	Friday	petak
Tuesday	utorak	Saturday	subota
Wednesday	sreda		

MONTHS

January	januar	July	jul
February	februar	August	avgust
March	mart	September	septembar
April	april	October	oktobar
May	maj	November	novembar
June	jun	December	decembar

NUMBERS

0	nula	18	osamnaest
1	jedan	19	devetnaest
2	dva	20	dvadeset
3	tri	21	dvadeset jedan
4	četiri	22	dvadeset dva
5	pet	30	trideset
6	šest	31	trideset jedan
7	sedam	40	četrdeset
8	osam	50	pedeset
9	devet	60	šezdeset
10	deset	70	sedamdeset
11	jedanaest	80	osamdeset
12	dvanaest	90	devedeset
13	trinaest	100	sto
14	četrnaest	101	sto jedan
15	petnaest	102	sto dva
16	šesnaest	500	pet stotina
17	sedamnaest	1,000	jedna hiljada

Index

An asterisk (*) next to a page number indicates a map reference. Where there are several page references, the one in bold type refers to the main entry.

INDEX